To MICHAEL –

Keep your cents +
the Dollars will
follow.

Best,

Ron
Delessa H

Bear Market Edition

Gents
with no
¢ents

A closer look at
Wall Street, its customers,
financial regulators,
and the media

Ron DeLegge II
with illustrations by Dave Clegg

HALF**FULL**
PUBLISHING GROUP

For information about special discounts for bulk purchases, please contact Half Full Publishing Group at bulksales@halffullpublishing.com.

Half Full Publishing Group can bring authors to your live event. For more information contact us at www.halffullpublishing.com.

First edition published in 2011 by Half Full Publishing Group.
ISBN: 978-0-9847199-0-7
Library of Congress Control Number: 2011942097

Illustrations by Dave Clegg.
Book design by Mark Ward.
Publishing strategy by Jennifer Ryan.

Printed in the United States of America

In memory of Louis and Red

*The information contained within this book,
while not guaranteed by us, was gathered from
authoritative sources whose extensive advice
has not been particularly useful.*

Contents

Acknowledgements

I'd like to thank the following individuals for their help with this book: Amy Rodriguez, Bill Stuart, Dave Clegg, Dan Dolan, Daryl Montgomery, Elise R. Kerr-Rodriguez, Andy Djukanovic, Gil Weinreich, John Gaertner, Rick Ferri, Rosanne Rodriguez, Russell Wild, George Milne, Lila Roehl, Louise Rodriguez, Mark Ward, Max Rottersman, Jennifer Ryan, Larry DeLegge, Ron DeLegge, Sr., Grisel and Frida. Your suggestions and words of encouragement made this book possible. Finally, I'd like to acknowledge the hard work of my editor, Donna Cheverton.

Preface

Most of us were taught never to judge a book by its cover. But with this particular one, you can. In fact, I encourage you to. From beginning to end, *Gents with No Cents* is drenched with erroneous theories, half-truths, and fuzzy math. But since Wall Street was my main data source, you can blame them.

This book almost never happened. And the fact that it did wasn't because of brilliant logistical planning. Like other daily occurrences in the financial markets and elsewhere, it was one of those unpredictable, random flukes. I like to refer to it as a "Black Piano from the Sky," which is an even rarer occurrence than the Black Swan many on Wall Street claim to follow.

From the time I began writing this book's very first sentence to its last, no mainstream book publishers wanted to touch it with a 1,000-foot pole. According to my rejection letters, they had more important things to publish like *How to Become an Instant Billionaire*, which is among the chief reasons I felt *Gents with No Cents* had an outside chance of succeeding. So, I rolled up my sleeves and went to work.

I felt it was a citizen's duty not to just describe Wall Street as it really is, but to uncover its root mentality, which hovers between lunacy and adolescence. Along the way, I encountered a whole mess of other people with the same psychotic mindset who effortlessly act out the part.

In contrast to my peers, I do not write from a pompous, omnipotent perspective, because I am nothing greater than an opinionated observer, and—at times—a hapless participant, and—depending on the day, an out-of-control madman.

As the cover indicates, this book is the "Bear Market" edition, which means the two bear markets we've experienced over the past decade are probably only practice runs for the *real* bear market. And I, like the rest of the population, won't be ready.

Any errors or omissions you come across are my fault along with any other convenient scapegoats that can be located.

Ron DeLegge II

December 2011

Chapter 1
In The Beginning...

The original title I selected for this book was *Gulliver's Travels*, but since it was already taken, I had to settle for *Gents with No Cents*. There are many places where I could have begun this book: for example, talking about the $35,000 toilet or the $6,000 shower curtain. However, in the interest of keeping your interest, I think we should save the fine art of showering and upper-class waste disposal for later.

For a while now, the author has been observing Wall Street's activities from a window desk with an unobstructed view of a parking lot. On his desk are pens, papers, a microphone and a computer plugged into the world's largest animal laboratory—the Internet. It is through this fantastic electronic network and others like it that Wall Street's business of bidding and asking along with buying and selling occurs. Other activities like bluffing and testifying occur, too, but are generally limited to physical settings like conference rooms and courtrooms.

Mixed in with this daily bustle is a lot of baloney—stockpiles of it—and that's what this book is about. As you may have noticed, Wall Street's baloney is bountiful even though the bacon in our wallets is much less so. Where did all that money vanish to? We will investigate this question and the other classifications of baloney so generously contributed by the customers, regulators, the media, and the general public.

As we go about our analysis, you will see the author has no special attachment to any schools of financial theory, and he is not employed by any secret resistance movements here or abroad.*

Stacked in the corner of my office floor are reams of conflicting data that will be used as grounds for argument, and, if necessary, counter arguments. I will attempt to turn these double negatives into positives, just as is done in math. Regarding the triple and quadruple negatives, I will probably impersonate the Powerful Money Men and play it by ear. The other missing pieces will be cobbled together with seasonally adjusted statements to add color.

Apologies and Pre-Apologies

Before we go any further, I'd like to get a few apologies out of the way. First, for any bankruptcy lawyers reading this, I'm sorry to report there will not be a Chapter 11 or 13. Nevertheless, you will be pleased to know Chapter 7 is packed with plenty of financial skirting strategies for your clients.

I would also like to apologize to all followers of technical analysis for only including two charts in the entire book. Trust me, if there's anybody who knows a picture is worth a thousand words it's me. And I can assure you it was my original intent to have two thousand pictures. Had it not been for cranky editors, I would have had all pictures and no text.

Perusing Financial Literature

Most books about investing and personal finance can be generally categorized as "I told you so," "Look at me, I'm rich," or "Look at you, you're a bum." There are also ungraceful groupings like "Let me make you rich right now, you bum."

Other financial literature will try to impress you with the authors' resumes or their vast collection of mansions around the world. I have a

---

*Please send your proposals directly to my legal counsel listed in Chapter 9.

few belongings but probably not enough to make a strong impression. As a result, I'm cornered into lowball tactics like charming the reader with my looks. Come to think of it, wasn't that the same way they pulled off that big IPO for a digital fruit market back in '99?

We should not forget about the financial paraphernalia that proposes to help you "get back to even." You'll notice these very books were written by the same experts who helped their readers to fall behind.

Lastly, there are other sub-categories like, "What went wrong" and "What went right," along with the dark but ever popular "In the long-run we're all dead." This type of financial literature usually has the words "Armageddon" or "destruction" somewhere in the titles. Not long after they've been published, most of these books can be found at the local swap meet for a buck. And in enough time, this one will probably join them.

As you'll soon discover, this book is shamefully absent of statistical evidence and academic proof. Even if we had all the important data plus all of the relevant footnotes, whatever data is not invalidated by the footnotes is voided in another study that we missed. For that reason, you will not read sentences like, "According a 25-year study conducted by such-and-such university, it was revealed that 4.2 percent of all publicly traded corporations are 37 percent more profitable than their peers, with the exception of the 287 companies that pay annual dividends of 5.6 percent or more."

Although numbers don't lie, it's rather annoying that they don't tell us absolutely everything we need to know. Maybe it's because 99 percent of all statistics only tell us 49 percent of the story. That means someone like me has to volunteer to explain for the rest of us the 51 percent part of the story that the stats don't cover. So, if I do happen to quote any statistics anywhere herein, I promise to only use the ones gathered from the finest textbooks in my personal collection. That's the top three percent!

Trees Don't Grow to the Sky

Wall Street's history can be traced to a sycamore tree where traders and speculators would gather to buy and sell securities. A weeping willow was briefly considered as "the spot," but its depressing posture was deemed unacceptable for drumming up new business. In time, a coffee house became the business meeting place and eventually led to the formation of the New York Stock Exchange. Of course, these were the sunny days before the words "trader" and "banker" became racial slurs.

While all the necessary rules for trading securities had been established, other bonus activities like forecasting and underwriting were added to the brokerage business, encompassing a comprehensive list of other unnecessary services. The original business plan was to conquer the universe, but, instead, it almost demolished everything including the field of finance.

Throughout its existence, Wall Street has always been a place where form over substance is both championed and rewarded. The seaside palaces should be proof enough, as is the block of multi-billion dollar burned-out customer accounts. And through it all, the ambitious goal of converting the entire physical world, bit-by-bit and piece-by-piece, into marketable securities rolls right along. Meanwhile, the displeasing results from this exercise repeat themselves with such fierce consistency that doubts are raised about the accuracy of authoritative statements like, "Past performance is not a guarantee of future results." Is it really so? Then why is there a cemetery in the heart of New York's financial district?

Forecasting Tomorrow

Dreaming is Wall Street's business—not lying, cheating, and stealing, as the angry documentaries dogmatically claim. Regardless of whether they are monsters or benefactors, the Street's inhabitants are all dreamers; otherwise they would not have chosen this line of work. Even when their dreams turn out to be nightmares, the hallucinations of great wealth and power for themselves, or their customers, never die.

After brief observation, you'll find the typical Wall Street citizen has so many opinions about the future that you'll wish you had not asked. The fantasy starts with an impressive hunch about the future of everything. From the rookie analyst to the chief investment officer to the night janitor, each has a wonderful premonition. Their viewpoints, no matter how radical, dull or dumb, will always get more publicity than the average Joe's opinion, but how do they compare in terms of precision? According to my records, the accuracy ratio for both groups is about the same—lousy. Whatever the case, the Street's general attitude is that they know something nobody else does, and that this is the hot stuff that will make them a killing.

Let's examine our first specimen: the narrowly focused prognosticator. Without any hesitancy, he will tell you where the stock market is headed. His opinions are based upon fundamental or technical analysis, and, in some cases, top secret methods used by the paramilitary underground. For these one-trick ponies, any discussion beyond the realm of stocks triggers heavy sweating and stage III paranoia.

In contrast, the more well-rounded seer has a variety of opinions on a variety of subjects. Along with the latest outlook for stocks, he can quote next quarter's corporate earnings and tell which political party will control the Oval Office for the next two terms. And with the slightest encouragement, he'll also tell you next year's PGA championship winner. Like the U.S. Treasury Secretary, he's an opinionated fellow, but with less power and money.

Will any of these intriguing forecasts come true? Some might, but most won't. More important, will anyone other than forecasters be able to profit from the advice?

We cannot criticize any of Wall Street's prophesiers for trying to help us, but a lack of effort isn't the problem. When it comes to the financial market's future or the prospective movements in any class of investments, they know exactly what we know—a whole lot of nothing. No deep investigation is needed to arrive at this conclusion. You can simply compare your own experience, other people's experience, or review the unflattering empirical data.

A prognosticator's sin is not fraud but rather the immature belief that financial markets are predictable through a careful study. They convince themselves that researching the rise and fall of corporations will give hints about a huge rally, an edge at making speculative bets pay off, or help to deliver a consistent return that beats everything. All of these things are verifiably unpredictable; yet coming to grips with this truth is impossible for a childish mind and even harder for a clinically deranged one.

My Blue Period

The personal experience I obtained on Wall Street began when I was a customer in 1988 and bought my first stock against the advice of my broker. The stock was immediately sold for a three dollar profit, which wasn't bad for a young inexperienced punk. Beyond this single trade, my market timing was impeccable in at least one other respect: I missed the 1987 crash by a few months.

Eight years later I returned to Wall Street, but this time as an investment broker, financial advisor, life counselor, or whatever they call themselves these days. I was trained to sell mutual funds, and so that's what I did. The goal of my work was to convince customers there were gobs of money to be made, and, in the process, to make sure they never found out there were also gobs to be lost.

Calling people from the phone book* was one of the first ways I learned to get customers. The problem was my competition was doing the same thing. So to improve my chances, I began calling the names that started with "Z" because my competitors were making calls in alphabetical order starting with "A." It didn't work.

Early on, I was given blank customer account applications, a stack of mutual fund prospectuses (thirty for my briefcase and one for my customers), and glossy brochures. I was instructed to talk about the fascinating charts with performance history dating back to 1924. I thought I was getting into the investment business, but it felt more like abstract expressionism, because the charts had all the graphical attributes of a Jackson Pollock painting. To this day, I'm still not sure if I was imitating art or it was imitating me.

It didn't take long to find out that my job wasn't so much about working *on* Wall Street as it was working *for* Wall Street. They needed some help selling harmless investment products, and I was happy to oblige. I needed the money, they needed the customers, and so we met three-quarters of the way in between.

The Hours

The U.S. stock market is open for business Monday through Friday from 9:30 a.m. to 4:00 p.m. (EST) and closed on every major holiday, with the exception of April Fools' Day. The nocturnal types unable to maintain this schedule will resort to after-hours trading, because if they're not in front of a computer screen by the stroke of midnight, they turn into pumpkins.

In the old days, traders would congregate on the stock exchange floor to conduct business. One man would yell stock prices to a group of

---

*For anyone under the age of 25, a phone book is a thickly printed volume that contains names, addresses, and telephone numbers. It's almost like Facebook, but without pictures.

men, they'd yell back, and no one would agree. Another group of men would interrupt the previous group's yelling with their own yelling, and securities transactions would get done. Nowadays, these rare face-to-face encounters still occur, but mostly at private cocktail receptions. Physical trading floors probably no longer need to exist, but they do, mainly to keep the racetracks empty during business hours.

The devolution of centralized trading floors has led to one other significant trend; it has given nosy media reporters a perch to broadcast from. Instead of pontificating from the stands like true bleacher bums, they do it right on the field. I seriously doubt floor traders and market specialists from previous generations would have allowed reporters to walk all over their turf as if they owned the joint. Would you want a camera pointing in your face as you're in the midst of fleecing whomever? Reporters should really be broadcasting from a server farm, because that's where all the real action in today's market is located.

Understanding the Lingo

If you ask Mr. Forecaster the basis of his financial outlook, there's a high probability that somewhere in his dissertation he will quote conventional wisdom. Boring as that may be, it is the safe thing to do and, furthermore, he's not programmed for anything else.

Here's a sample of financial thinking he's likely to utter, along with a general translation:

"Buy on the dips" is widely circulated advice that says you should purchase any security that has fallen in price because eventually it will go back up. The phrase was originally coined as just "buy the dips," but when the sales for sour cream dips surged uncontrollably, it was abruptly modified to "buy *on* the dips." Since the change, the profits once enjoyed by sour cream makers have been re-routed to Wall Street.

Wall Streeters who haven't kept up with their continuing education courses can still be heard saying "Buy the dips." And when they do, guess what happens? Sales for sour cream dips instantaneously jumps.

The saying "Gentlemen prefer bonds" was first pronounced by American banker Andrew W. Mellon who said it in the 1930s as he was protesting the rising tax burdens of the rich. In 1953, Hollywood got hold of it and turned it into a movie called "Gentlemen Prefer Blondes."

Today, this charming old proverb has been readopted by corporate executives and Wall Street types everywhere but in a slightly altered format: "Gentlemen prefer bail bonds."

Another curious motto is to "Sell down to the sleeping point," which suggests a strong connection between investing and sleeping. It basically means the holdings inside your investment portfolio should never interfere with your sleeping schedule. Insomniacs, are you listening?

What about investors who have already fallen asleep? How is it possible for them to "sell down to the sleeping point" if they're already in a state of unconsciousness? I don't know the answer to that question; better ask the people who came up with it.

Valuation Techniques

It's a little early to be talking about valuing businesses, but let's take a shot at the subject. If we're wrong, we can always correct ourselves later.

Let's begin our journey into price and value by analyzing one of the most familiar technology companies across the globe. The stock is Apple, formerly referred to as Apple Computer and today known as "Mac," "AAPL," or "iPad" by its many groupie followers.

First, let's discuss the price, about which I am very knowledgeable. I can state without any hesitancy that Apple shares closed yesterday at $374.93* with a final bid of $374.86 and a final ask at $374.99. That price

*Source: The Internet.

was determined because at 4 p.m. yesterday someone was willing to pay $374.86 for at least 100 shares of Apple while someone else was willing to sell it for $374.99. The identity of the people behind this buying and selling was not revealed, so it could have been anyone from your father-in-law to your boss or a similarly dislikeable creature. In other words, the price of Apple's stock was established in a very iffy manner. The good thing we can say about that price, though, is that it was a concrete figure, and it was valid everywhere at a specific moment in time.

Now, let's examine value. Apple's earnings have been dynamite, but what if they suddenly veer in the wrong direction? What if a competitor invents better products and services? Worse yet, what if management turns the cash cow into a snake pit? Other doubts linger. Does Junior really need another electronic device? Aren't the four he already has enough? And besides that, who will be able to afford these earthly possessions, let alone the never-ending subscription fees, should the economy worsen? It just goes to prove how foolish a price of $374.93 for Apple's stock is, because $37.93 is more like it, and anyone who pays more than that with anything except frequent flier miles should be checked into the nearest psychiatry ward.

But from another angle, there are many relevant points our prior analysis may have missed. Technology is one of the fastest growing industry sectors, and the growth of its combined market size over the past 25 years goes without saying. Technology is not just business—it has become the very engine of business! And Apple is the cream of the crop, a fierce competitor with an innovative spurt that matches in length your favorite CEO's deposition. Furthermore, it sits on roughly $76 billion* in cash—and cash, as they say—is king. In view of this aspect and other bullish factors, it's difficult to understand why this gem of a company

---

*That figure was before management's ghoulish spending spree.

is not selling for $974.93 per share. And who shall dare call us nuts for rounding up to a $1,000?

After considering this spectrum of convincing arguments, the entire subject of price and value is as clear as mud. So to settle the question once and for all, I'll offer up a real life case of an elderly man who was embroiled in a financial dispute.

The man was being bothered by his daughters because his home had fallen into disrepair, and they were trying to show him the place was a money pit. According to them, it was time to sell and move out, but the old coot wouldn't budge. Finally, the man spoke. "Enough!" he said. "It took me 50 years to pay off this house. Look at it. It has hot water, electricity, and indoor plumbing. If apartments on Park Avenue with this same stuff are priced for millions, what do you think this place is *really* worth?"

When the Bull Bumped into a Black Swan

Up until now, I've made an energetic attempt to avoid any mythological references, but my efforts to cease and desist are hopeless. I blame my lack of self-control on financial philosophers whose paganism has devoured me. The various deities, which were formally just bulls and bears, have been expanded to include rogue birds.

A Black Swan occurrence is a rare and highly unexpected event with extraordinary implications. For instance, receiving a thank you card from the IRS is a Black Swan occasion with magnificent repercussions. Aside from being totally unexpected, it has the potential to breathe life back into the U.S. Post Office. Just imagine!

More frequently, the Black Swan theory is applied to financial markets. According to legend, things like a stock market crash, a housing bust, an economic collapse and so forth, occur—not because of perfectly insane people or upset bears—but because of *geese*. Put your calculators away!

What happens when the black swan is taken by surprise?

Who knew that finding the true reasons behind these mind-boggling events would be easy as pi.

But before the Black Swan ever landed inside theorists' brains, it was preceded by a Black Piano from the sky. What happens when the Black Piano or a flock of them annihilates the Swan with a surprise crash landing? Do financial markets stop existing? And if they do, how are we supposed to cash in our winning chips?

A Word to the Wise

The remainder of this book will be spent studying the hysterical tendencies of people. The other items, like profits and losses, are just filler. For those of us who already know everything there is to know about Wall Street and money, I'll try not to confuse you with the facts.

In the final chapter, you will be given an opportunity to add your two cents to this manuscript. Like the holder of an options contract, you will be granted the right, not the obligation, to participate, and I will do everything in my power to agitate you toward that end. Should you choose the path of participation, you might even hit the jackpot. Of course, that's assuming a jackpot still exists.

fall furiously. The executive team was nevertheless pleased because they had followed the best practices outlined in their company's Policies and Procedures Manual, which states to always have lots of meetings.

Business 101

The purpose of a business is not limited to a place where resumes are simply collected and kept on file. Nor is it a place where appetizing mission statements are merely hatched. A business is a genuine adult playground, with running, throwing, kicking, flirting, fighting, and crying. Interspersed among these daily happenings are other bonus activities like typing, printing, emailing, and conference calling. Above all, business is a sanctuary where incompetence and insanity are permitted to be called talent and skill.

As much of a platform for showcasing one's abilities that a business can be, it can also serve to conceal assets and private affairs. In times of need, a business can be used as collateral. And in times of greed, a business can be used as a personal ATM. A business is a soulless entity that commits no sins but gets all the blame.

What is the *real* purpose of a business? It depends on who you ask. To the cynic, the purpose of a business is to populate the planet with inhumane sub-humans. To the idealist, the corporation's chief reason for existence is to be profitable. While the latter view is probably the right one, it unfairly omits a lot of misinformation.

The Conglomerates

In evaluating businesses, we might as well start with the cream of the crop—conglomerates.

This group of enterprises is far-reaching, with many sub-divisions within sub-divisions that also have plenty of their own sub-divisions. Besides keeping potential competitors at bay, conglomerates are so large that they keep employees from knowing what the other employees are

Welcome to our corporate headquarters.
Doorbell broken, please knock.

doing. Accumulating all of these companies can take many decades, and successfully integrating them can take even longer. After a while, the whole thing begins to resemble the Windsor family tree.

Under ideal circumstances, a successful* conglomerate will have many business units as different and far removed from each other as the sun and the moon. Each of these businesses will offset the others to produce one giant happy return. When they don't, they'll typically produce one giant migraine. Problematic as this may sound, it is nothing that a capable management consulting firm—after thousands of hourly billings—can't partially fix.

Even with all of their operational difficulties, conglomerates are still an impressive collectible. The premise behind them is to create a company so large and vast that it lives on perpetually. However, when a conglomerate topples, it eliminates not just itself but anything within 24,000 miles.

The Executive's Mindset

Preserved deep within a corporation's bowels is an extraordinary creature unlike any other—the corporate executive. Before you've even started your day, he has already been on a three-hour conference call with Asia about a big merger. Before that, he was yelling at Europe while you were tucking in the kids. Most people sleep when they sleep, but he works. The corporate executive is not a lazy man.

In our examination of corporate executives, we must remember to never judge. We must also remember that a stereotype is not a stereotype, especially if it's true.

Inside the executive's subconscious mind (yes, even business people have a conscience) are his stock options vesting schedule, his getaway strategy from whatever and whomever, and maybe even a mistress. She

---

*The adjective "successful" in this context is misplaced, but I couldn't think of anything else.

will meet him for dinner because, as always, the company is buying. He's at the top of his game.

Certain chief executives rise above the rest for the sole purpose of crucifying the competition. As much fun as that may be, some executives are more enthralled with persecuting shareholders and business partners than competitors. A psychologist might say that malice is the foundation of the executive's character, but the executive doesn't see it that way. His enthusiasm is merely misinterpreted as rage and his generosity as manslaughter. He works, not because he has to, but to escape the rat race of golfing and fishing. Nobody understands him—including himself.

Contrary to what the tabloids say, the corporate executive is a family person. Whenever there's a graduation or funeral, he always sends a check. He's ethical, principled and decent—according to his legal counsel. In his free time, which is never, he obtains great motivation from reading literature written by the Great Business Thinkers.* Maybe he's morally challenged, but he's not necessarily evil. He's an incurable romantic; otherwise, he would not be where he is today.

What about executive pay? What about it! Look at the individuals who are complaining about executive pay. Aren't they the same group who celebrates when their favorite sports team signs a $300 million ballplayer? What's more important—putting a ball into play or testifying before Congress? (*Touché* if your answer was "neither," you hopeless cynic.)

Most complaints about executive compensation, in my opinion, are overstated. Never discussed in these criticisms are the rising cost of keeping jet aircraft, personal chefs, mansions, and other boisterous fluff. Do you really think a minimum wage salary is going to cover the private island's mortgage payment? Memo to everyone: Living like a mogul isn't cheap, and, unfortunately, new accounting rules don't allow for any of

*See *Stink and Grow Rich* by Napoleon Shill.

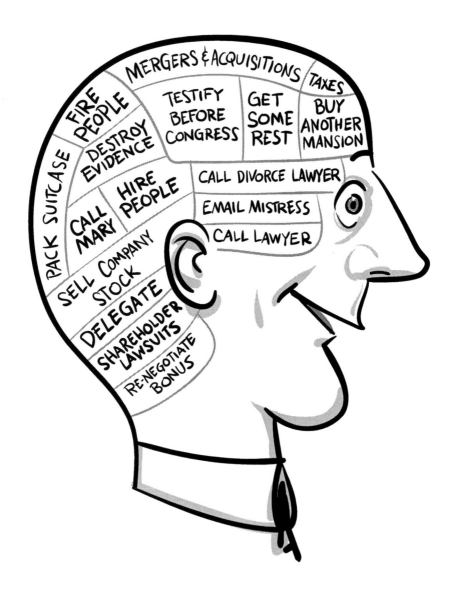

The corporate executive's mind.

*Can I please get the skirt and pinstriped suit
with the hot air?*

these unnecessary items to be designated as off-balance sheet expenditures. (Enron really messed things up.) If shareholders aren't going to pony up, who will?

On a positive note, I'm pleased to report the national uproar surrounding executive pay has since subsided into a smaller-scaled uproar with scattered incidents of civil disobedience. Threats were made and a few windows were broken, but no mortalities—other than shareholders who died from shock—were recorded. Let's make a documentary!

If you would still like to protest CEO pay, I would, too. I'll meet you in front of the New York Stock Exchange tomorrow at noon. I nominate you to cast the first stone.

From Executive to Diplomat

Naturally, the curious bystander wants to know, "Where do corporate executives come from, and who is responsible for educating them?" It was my original intention to list their parents by name, but cataloging family patriarchs and matriarchs would create an additional 156 pages of wasted space. This predicament left me with no choice but to analyze their resumes.

Although falsifying information on a resume is widely considered a taboo business practice, today it has become so commonplace that it's almost taboo not to do it. In fact, bogus resumes have gotten so out of hand that they are the third leading cause for CEO firings, right behind illicit office affairs and going to prison.

In this regard, let me offer all corporate executives two rules of thumb: First, residing in the same city as a particular university does not automatically make you an alumnus of that university; second, if you cannot remember the name of the university you attended, it's best to focus on your other strengths, like the one time you increased profits two percent by cutting your company's workforce 87 percent.

Finally, if you're convinced you attended a particular university but are unsure whether or not you received a diploma, call the school immediately and ask for the registrar's office. Should the registrar refuse to acknowledge your token commitment to the educational process, agree to make a generous donation and see if the university will give you an honorary degree. (Not a decree, a *degree*.) Then, once you receive your diploma, you can tell everyone that you're a diplomat. Do it for alma mater—even if you don't have one!

Directing and Acting

As time passed, it was determined that corporate America needed more accountability. Someone, other than a federal judge and ankle monitors, should supervise the kids running the show. Someone should also be responsible for doling out the golden parachutes, golden handcuffs, and golden coffins. This process eventually led to the formation of corporate boards, also known as the "board of directors."

A lot of hot air has been wasted on this subject, so I'd like to add to it.

Some of the most outstanding examples of self-dealing and nepotism can be found in the corporate board room. But don't confuse a little favoritism for something it is not: a "conflict of interest." More on that in a moment.

What is a board of directors? It's a tight knit association of two or more bureaucrats, but fewer than fifty. In the business world the members are typically referred to as "directors," although, in truth, they do more acting than directing.

Corporate directors carry on many fundamental tasks, which include showing up late for quarterly meetings, re-hiring the wrong people, and defending their bureaucracy.* If time allows, they'll talk about other trivial

---

*For further study on techniques in evasion see *The Act of War* by Sun Tzu.

matters, like stock performance, lowering executives' compensation, and the firing of incompetent managers.

And now, the most wonderful part of becoming a directing actor: The work schedule.

Normally, directors are asked to attend just four whole meetings per year. (Really demanding companies require directors to attend more meetings than that, for which they receive an additional generosity fee.) Assuming they don't sleep at meetings, this time amounts to less than two months of "work" for the entire year.

How many acts of gross negligence have been committed in the name of corporate governance? The official figure is unavailable, but, thankfully, wiretaps can't penetrate the mahogany paneling.

None of these occupational hazards should ever dissuade you from trying your hand as a corporate director, if given the chance. Acting and directing pays! And if it doesn't, then the insurance company will pay. Three cheers for D&O liability insurance!

Finally, let's talk about a much discussed but little understood thing called "conflicts of interest."

Let's suppose a corporate director has a son-in-law who is acting as the company's CEO, which is not necessarily a conflict of interest, but it could be. If the son-in-law also carries his father-in-law's golf clubs and drives his fourth Mercedes, deep suspicion is raised. That example is a definite conflict of interest, but even more, it's also an interesting conflict. Furthermore, it can pay handsome dividends, so long as nobody finds out.

As you've just learned, conflicts of interest can be interesting conflicts, but they are rarely just "conflicts." I define a real conflict as any activity where you would be considered subordinate to your mother-in-law. Talk about trouble!

*Can I please get the skirt and pinstriped suit
with the hot air?*

Corporate Bailouts

The rules concerning financial bailouts for failing corporations have recently been completely rewritten, not because of an oversight, but due to the fact that previous bailout rules were never written. Consequently, government bailouts for corporate America are best explained in an ancient story of man versus fire.

Once upon a time, a man without any homeowners insurance lost his home to a fire. He was suspected of setting the home ablaze, but, with some legal coaching, he neither admitted nor denied the allegations. He filed a claim with a few different insurance companies, demanding payment or else. Mind you, he was never entitled to insurance coverage for various reasons, from not paying any premiums to being the prime suspect in the destruction of his own home.

In any case, the insurance companies, frightened by the unknown consequences of his "or else" ultimatum, promptly paid the man's insurance claim. Meanwhile, the cost of everyone else's homeowners insurance was increased by 70 percent. The End.

In this parable, the man stands for corporate officials, the insurance company is the government and everyone else is you and me. The corporation is represented by the home, and the 70 percent increase in homeowners insurance illustrates rising taxes.

Beyond this little anecdote, the juvenile tactics employed in obtaining bailout winnings from the U.S. government is unchartered territory, even for this book. Therefore, I won't discuss them.

How to Identify "Talent"

In Hollywood, "talent" was once defined as someone who could entertain an audience by singing, acting, and dancing. The majority of today's so-called movie stars only know how to act, and many are questionable at that.

On Wall Street, I figure there are actually three sub-divisions of talent: There's undiscovered talent, untapped talent, and raw talent. What are their differences? Someone who supervises more than a billion dollars of losses in any given year has untapped talent. On the other hand, someone who can single-handedly tip the entire global financial system upside down has raw talent. Finally, undiscovered talent refers to someone who has the former capabilities, but hidden away.

There's another group of "talented" souls we should not overlook.

What about the people who can pass a lie detector test on the first try? Or, what about the individuals who ricochet from one office tower to the next, yet always land on their feet? How about those who can effortlessly extract blood from a turnip? And let us not overlook the other Wall Street "talents," the ones who can accurately guess fourth quarter earnings in the first quarter with 20/20 hindsight vision.

The other lower level "talents" know how to successfully match a bathing suit with Gucci loafers. Just below this group are the lesser "talented" souls who can redecorate an office suite that doesn't even need redecorating on a $1.2 million shoestring budget.

Shareholders – A Portrait

In an effort to explain why publicly traded companies have not lived up to their theoretical promise, I have thus far only mentioned their liabilities. This is hardly a fair method for consideration, so let's look at another aspect of a business—the owners.

Shareholders are the mythical people from a far-away land who own the company. Without them, the petty atrocities that surround us would be unachievable. While shareholders are frequently portrayed as victims, they also double as stealth accomplices.

The various shareholder personalities that exist will generally follow that of Snow White's Seven Dwarfs: Bashful, Sleepy, Sneezy, Dopey, Happy, Grumpy and Doc.

Shareholder sightings are rare but can sometimes occur at shareholder meetings. The few shareholders who are gutsy enough to show up usually temper their nerves by remaining completely silent. After the meeting has ended, they return to their far-away-places, satisfied that they have accomplished something meaningful.

Troublemakers are another type of shareholder.

As fanatical offshoots of Grumpy, they make it their duty to oppose any and all recommendations made by the company's management. They attend shareholder meetings not to listen and learn, but to demand and disrupt. If there's time, they'll refuse to sit down after several commands to do so.

This dissident shareholder makes powerful demands such as, "Why hasn't the company been sold yet? Or why don't my 21 shares have more voting rights?" After these questions have been ignored, other profound inquiries follow. "When are we going to execute another stock split? Why can't we have shareholder meetings closer to a good shopping mall or near a golf course?"

"Shareholder Value"

Although it doesn't seem like it, much of the business conducted on Wall Street is done with a real purpose. And the oft-cited reason is to deliver "shareholder value." Since the true definition of shareholder value is open for debate, I'll take a stab with a true story.

A certain publicly traded company was experiencing declining revenue, declining profits, and a declining share price. Executives scrambled to find a solution but were at odds with large shareholders on which recovery path to take. Both sides continued to privately and publicly undermine each other, disagreeing on almost everything. Therapy anyone?

The company's problems were very complicated, so a multi-pronged answer was needed. To that end, executives took drastic cost-cutting measures by banning the office usage of paper clips, rubber bands, and staples. Rolling electricity blackouts were also added in order to reduce the company's overhead even further. Mass layoffs were tried, but when the employees' union objected, salaries were cut instead. For their ideas, each of the executives was awarded with an additional allotment of fully-vested stock options. How did the market react?

Although the executive stock options diluted existing shareholders by 43 cents per share, the company had just "saved" ten cents, thereby creating additional "shareholder value," according to the press release. To celebrate their accomplishment, executives were invited to a bell ringing ceremony. For a brief moment, the company's stock price was lifted, and its shareholders were happy. Another sheep had been shorn, but who knew?

Day at the Office with Fibonacci

Corporate accounting should be a matter of simple addition, subtraction, multiplication, and division, but General Accepted Account Principles (GAAP) disallows a straightforward process. For this reason, there are various accounting methods we will need to examine together.

Examples of popular bean-counting strategies include aggressive accounting, creative accounting, cooking the books, and, finally, shredding the books. Beyond these methods, corporate accounting can be divided into three general categories: 1) accounting to keep the regulators happy, 2) accounting to keep shareholders happy, and 3) accounting to keep auditors from going out of business. Each constituency has different needs and accounting standards that can be easily adjusted (north or south, east or west) to meet those needs.

For businesses with inventory, FIFO (first in, first out) and LIFO (last in, first out) are two familiar accounting methods; thankfully, neither one involves burning down the warehouse. Since the 1970s, U.S. companies have favored the usage of LIFO. Coincidentally, LIFO is also the preferred method of imprisonment by criminal defense attorneys for their corporate clients.

In the 1990s, Internet based businesses introduced clicks, visits, and eye-balls into the accounting vernacular. More recently, this unsavory practice has greatly declined after one venture backed company was caught double counting eyeballs with contact lenses.

To learn further how contemporary accounting came to be, we must look back to the 13th Century, which brings us to the Italian mathematician Fibonacci's* era.

Fibonacci taught the world about the orderliness of numbers. And, while his numerical system is typically applied to financial graphs and other incomprehensible minutiae, it comes in rather handy for basic accounting applications.

Of particular interest is the correct sequence of numbers, which nobody seems to remember anymore. Here it is: 1, 2, 3, 4, 5, 6, 7, 8, 9, 10, 11, 12, etc. Don't bother studying Fibonacci's other work, especially his numerical sets that bounce all over the place like Mexican jumping beans, until you have first mastered the basics.

The Big Idea

Since 2001, a convincing argument could be made that accounting is neither an art nor a science but is instead an abstract illusion. In that year there arose a magnificent accounting scandal that took Enron from

---

*His other lesser known nickname was "Fibber."

class genius to world class blockhead. Before then, the company had flourished like a magical beanstalk by using assets people thought existed, but didn't. While this type of demented thinking has produced many well-received white papers, it has also put a few corporations and their auditors into hot water. How do you think the Big 8 became the Little 27?

Interestingly, some corporations have sought to apply the "Enron technique" for dealing with gross accounting errors. Like Rickey Henderson, they're in the stolen base business. Spreadsheets are neatly printed onto a few reams of paper and then inserted into whatever paper shredders will eat them. Accounting software is deleted and computers are donated to Goodwill.* Once these steps are completed, auditors are called in and paid a consulting bribe. Eventually, the math works itself out, and whatever irregularities that remain are for the next management team to worry about.

Maybe the trouble with accountants and accounting isn't a mathematical problem, but one of linguistics. At this point, the subject should be passed off to the English teachers.

The word "accountant" is actually derived from two root words: "to count" and "ant." Put another way, accountant literally translates as "to count very little." Mathematically speaking, here's the equation: Accountant + Accounting = Little Counting.

At first glance, this provocative formula doesn't look right because it goes against everything we've been told about accountants and their numbers. On the positive side, it supports a good conspiracy crutch that rogue software is to blame for paranormal occurrences, like beating analysts' earnings estimates by a penny for 32 straight quarters. Asimov's robots are on the loose again. Help!

---

*I did not say computers are counted as "goodwill." I said they are contributed *to* Goodwill.

A Boy Named Sue

By now, all the mathematical possibilities of accounting have been fully explored and tried by corporate America. Just one item is left—the balance sheet.

This particular document is the guts of the corporation, even when it bears a greater resemblance to a skeleton. The balance sheet is designed to explain the company's financial condition by listing alien concepts such as assets, liabilities, and owner's equity. In contrast, off-balance-sheet activities contain these very same items but are only disclosed if they are an immediate threat to a few hundred million people.

Hasn't it been repeatedly shown that balance sheets are the furthest thing from being balanced? Aren't there better names for a balance sheet than a "balance" sheet? I nominate a different name, something more fitting, like "table of contents," "bucket list," or "cookbook."

Foreshadowing this trapeze act was one American businessman's decision to select "National Amusements" as the name of his privately held company. Apparently, "National Gag" and "National League" weren't catchy enough. With the help of branding consultants, he determined that "National Amusements" was a more accurate reflection of the business climate.

One More Try

If you still want to understand more about the mathematics of corporate accounting, perhaps this story will help.

A certain CEO was interviewing job applicants for the position of CFO. He devised a bullet-proof test to select the most suitable individual for the job. He asked each applicant, "What is two plus two?"

The first applicant was a journalist who answered, "Twenty-two."

The second applicant was an engineer: "According to my scientific calculator, the correct answer is between 3.999 and 4.001."

The next person was a lawyer who stated that, in the case of Albright vs. Smith, two plus two was proven to be four.

The last applicant was an accountant. The CEO asked, "How much is two plus two?" The accountant rose from his chair, went to the door, closed it, came back, and sat down. Leaning across the desk and in a low voice, he said, "Sir, how much do you want it to be?"

Needless to say, the accountant won the job and enjoyed a long, profitable career. The company's shareholders weren't as fortunate.

Our Collector's Edition

There are many misstatements, half-truths, and other erroneous declarations in this particular chapter, but I have the numbers to back them up. If you are still unsatisfied with my figures, I can always restate them later, similar to the way corporate earnings are reported at a few publicly traded companies we know.

I hope what I've written does not skew your opinion about the fine reputation of business and everything it has to offer. In fact, three weeks ago was a great time to invest. Sure the market went down a little*, but our contacts in Washington D.C. rescued us, so we got the heck out. Despite a few lost belongings, we managed to keep an exclusive list of 12 publicly-traded stocks with all the attributes you seek. The list will be part of our yet-to-be-released collector's edition and is only available for purchase by the first eight million people.

In the meantime, should you think for whatever reason that today's corporations or their business executives are utterly atrocious, just wait until you meet their successors.

---

*In this context, the definition of a "little" is not "a lot." What's a lot? Any amount that's more than a little.

Chapter 3
Customers—That Venturesome Bunch

Most of the daily nonsense that occurs on Wall Street today would not be possible without customers. A customer can be informally defined as anyone who is willing to throw down some money. Some customers are big and some are small, but, regardless of how much money they have, the propensity to self-destruct is a constant.

I'm not entirely certain the word "customer" can fully describe the process of people turning their money loose to Wall Street's financial wizards. I think fans, volunteers, stunt people, guinea pigs, sacrificial lambs, and plaintiffs are all much better descriptions. Let's take a random walk down Main Street to learn more about them.

A Diversity of Customers

People with a bright ray of hope aren't the only kinds of customers. There are institutional investors who have large sums to play with. This group encompasses banks and insurance companies along with college endowments, foundations, and pension funds. They make splendid customers, if you can get them.

Other customers are high net worth families and private trusts. Usually, someone in the family has some sort of experience with the stock market and can talk off your ear about the right way to allocate $7 million. Absent of these know-it-alls are the other large customer accounts with so many layers it is hard to tell the top from the bottom. Which gatekeeper of gatekeepers knows how to reach the boss's boss? And once you do reach the boss's boss, are you sure you've got the right boss?

The vast majority of customers are individuals who run the gamut from rich people and business owners all the way to mom and pop investors. At the bottom of the heap are customers with small accounts that nobody wants. A fee of one percent on a $3,500 account is only $35 a year. No serious broker or advisor wants to have that sort of responsibility, so the customer is promptly sold an annuity that pays the salesperson a nine percent commission. If the customer is lucky, he can withdraw all his money without penalties in 15 years. By then, the insurance company that issued the original annuity contract has changed names a half dozen times.

Common Species

The first type of customer is not really a customer but a *prospective* customer who typically has money to invest—an undetermined amount—that is construed to be a significant number. Financial institutions, advisors, and brokers drool over them, but, like a voluptuous young lady, this type of prospective customer is extremely elusive and rare. At times, they are so difficult to come across it's believed they've gone into extinction like the Australian Thylacine. But a bull market brings them out of hibernation and they begin to surface like a large school of jellyfish. And, anyone who can extract more than $1,000 from them to invest in the market is a fortunate person.

In my former life as a financial advisor, here are the other customer types that I encountered:

Ape People

These are the obsessive types that attempt to mimic the financial transactions of well-known investors. Over the years, Warren Buffett has been a popular target for Ape People. "If Buffett can become a billionaire

But the billboard outside said I would win!?!

by investing in just a handful of individual stocks, why can't I?" they reason. So Ape People convince themselves they can achieve billionaire status by imitating Buffett's every move. In spite of these decent efforts, Ape People are not billionaires, nor are they close.

Beach Bums

Look at them. How do you *think* they invest? They're beach bums. Need I say more?

Conspiracy Boobs

Anything bad that happens to a Conspiracy Boob is because of behind-the-scenes puppetry by hidden forces. Boobs are experts at finding someone to blame. Whether it is marketplace manipulation—real or imagined—or other excuses, Boobs know exactly why their investment accounts are down 62 percent: It's everyone else's fault!

The Conspiracy Boob enjoys feeding himself with gloomy entertainment. The rest of the world likes a good romance with a happy ending, but the Boob prefers death poems by Edgar Allan Poe. In time, these customer types eventually boycott the stock market.

My data shows Conspiracy Boobs are not very good investment clients to have, unless you happen to be a Boob just like them. I know from firsthand experience these types of customers are not interested in obtaining profitable investment returns, because their main goal is revenge.

Day Traders

Day traders are known for their rapid fire buying and selling. They're inclined to trade any securities with a standard deviation of zip, bang, and boom. It's not uncommon for these trades to end badly, but like a Timex watch, traders take a licking and keep on ticking.

Day traders, according to habit, are allergic to financial concepts like diversification and asset allocation. Usually within a few hours of buying a stock, the typical day trader succumbs to the seven-year itch and feels the urgent need to sell. To be caught holding a mixture of neatly arranged investments is unimaginable.

In my earliest days in the securities business, I was warned about trying to get day traders as customers. My manager explained it to me this way: "Son, do you have any idea about the difference between government bonds and day traders? The difference is government bonds pay income and eventually mature."

Ex-customer Customers

These are the folks who in one way or another have been burned. Whether the burning was self-inflicted or administered by someone else, they vow never to invest another nickel in the stock market.

Where do ex-customer customers put their money? It can be in just about anything—except evil securities—including the sofa cushion underneath their rumps.

Oddly, I've known many ex-customer customers who have made it a habitual practice of returning to the same godforsaken sources that got them into trouble. These kinds of customers do not need a good financial plan; they need a good psychiatrist.

Gamblin' Geezers

You've met these types of people at the local store. They're the elderly folk holding up the line because they want to buy lottery ticket numbers that match the birthdays of their 18 grandchildren.

What do their investment portfolios look like? They have seven shares of this, 34 shares of that, three shares of this, 26 shares of that, and so forth. To evaluate this type of portfolio, don't bother using Monte Carlo software—I recommend a kaleidoscope.

The Gamblin' Geezers are likely to have the investment mix of sixteen-year-old teenagers. They're not playing the stock market sweepstakes to make money, but rather, they are trying to reclaim their youth.

Noncommittal Flirts

These are the individuals with two or more financial advisors. If you ask them why they've hired multiple counselors, they'll explain to you it's because they are comparing results and that you would be wise to try the same thing. Their money is the testing ground for the unusual results that typically follow.

Generally speaking, Flirts are excellent customers for one or two quarters and then they bail. If they stay longer than that, it's probably because they're being hustled with fruit baskets, Super Bowl tickets, and other free stuff.

Radical Conservatives

A Radical Conservative is anyone who gets motion sickness from standing still. These types of customers will usually own a savings account, while the more aggressive ones will break down and buy a certificate of deposit (CD).

On more than one occasion, I made the mistake of trying to get Radical Conservatives to sell their CDs and to invest in something more promising. In every single case, they were immediately crushed by a severe bout of separation anxiety.

Bankers should be fully aware of the Radical Conservatives' strict dietary preferences. They enjoy burned coffee with powered cream and stale cookies. Do not make the mistake of inviting them to a steakhouse, because they're more than satisfied eating off twice-used paper plates from the bank's lobby.

See what I hooked?! It's a whale of a fish too—
my biggest catch ever!

Sophisticated Types

Inspired in part by Duke Ellington's "Sophisticated Lady," the sophisticated investor, by definition, is a high net worth individual who has enough money to absorb losses that would make the average citizen instantly bankrupt.

Another tell-tale sign of sophisticated investors is that they have several financial institutions stalking them. To see sophisticated investors firsthand, go to any upscale hotel lobby and look around. A sophisticated investor can locate the concierge desk wearing a blindfold. Observe carefully, because you'll see them.

Getting Customers

The next two questions we bump into are: How does Wall Street get its customers? And from where do customers come?

Let's tackle the first question. There are many strategies for getting customers. You can bribe them, tease them, romance them, hound them, threaten them, feed them, seduce them, sell them, trick them, date them, and if things go really well, marry them. While I have no comment about the success rate of these methods, I've seen some financial advisors do all of them during the same presentation.

Among the more difficult methods for getting new customers are being at the right country club at the right time, or running into a group of fabulously wealthy citizens who know absolutely nothing about money but who are willing to give you a try.

Over the past several years, free meal seminars have become quite popular. I've known certain financial professionals who could feed an army of retirees but who couldn't feed their own families. Prospective clients eat lobster and steak while the spouse and kids get peanut butter and jelly. This method for getting clients has done an outstanding job at fostering a culture of freeloaders.

These occupational hazards are common to the investment business. After kissing enough of the wrong prospects, many advisors end up with a bad case of mononucleosis.

The final question pertains to where customers come from, which reminds me of a similar inquiry aimed at parents: "Mommy, daddy, where do babies come from?" Without getting into the gross and confusing details, I'll err on the side of simplicity: Customers, like babies, are delivered in a basket by a white stork from the sky.

Getting a Customer's Attention

Few things anywhere can captivate the attention of the investing public like the occurrence of jumbo-sized dividends. While not officially illegal, there's nevertheless something strikingly adulterous about a stock that pays a double digit yield or some other absurdly bloated figure.

What if you encounter a stock with a gluttonous yield? Here is the meaning, based upon my in-depth research: 1) The stock's dividend is a misprint; 2) The stock has a zero chance of going up, 3) The stock is very close to being delisted and/or; 4) The stock's juicy dividend is on the verge of being cut or completely eliminated by management because it can't be sustained.

What should you do if your stock's dividend has been abruptly axed? I wish I had better news, but there's nothing more permanent than a temporary dividend cut. In the meantime, try not to panic. Management is aware of the problem and plans on resuming dividend payments as soon as possible, which is probably never. If you're agreeable, your dividends can be paid in the form of more company stock, what do say?

If you still don't understand any of this, I wrote a poem that may help:

My dividends have been cut. Now what?
I'm gettin' less money and it ain't funny

Is this what I get for chasing high yields?
I'm selling my penthouse to move into the fields

What kind of fair weather friend have you become?
I was baggin' 15 percent, but my stock has lost more than a ton

Who signed me up for this terrible deal?
Maybe it was the advisor who bought me that meal.

I've lost a bundle chasing dividends, I'm confessin'.
When besides never will I learn my lesson?

If money can't buy happiness, can high dividends?
My wallet is thinner, I've been kicked in the shins!

Oh dear dividends, where have you gone?
You used and abused me like your little pawn

I promise not to be your fool anymore
But not until after I settle the score

Just a little more pain might bring me some gain,
And our downsized lifestyle, I'll need not explain

Oh dear dividends, you've been forgiven
Just promise me and the family that you'll keep givin'

OK?

As our poem illustrates, the finest things in life, including high dividends, are fraught with lousy guarantees and have short-lived tendencies. The most successful approach to investing in high-dividend paying stocks is to not count on them. Put another way, I encourage you to find other ways of achieving disappointment.

"Dear Lover…"

Many customers have gotten themselves into a pickle for making the most innocent of all rookie mistakes: responding to emails that promise untold sums of great riches. These scheming emails will generally have the following words in the subject line: "Dear Winner," "Dear Beneficiary," and, in some explicit cases, they will say "Dear Lover."

Warning: You should not, under any circumstances, respond to the "Dear Winner" or "Dear Beneficiary" emails unless they happen to be from the King of Polynesia's bereaved brother, mother or son. (Regarding the "Dear Lover" emails, I cannot give you any advice in this area, other than to say don't do something that would get you into deep trouble with your real lover.) Should the email ask for your bank or brokerage account number or any other personal data, do not, no matter how tempting it may be, give it to them.*

Likewise, if they agree to send you 500 million Tögrög via international wire, tell them you appreciate the offer, but you only accept hand-delivered cash to your neighbor's backdoor. Your final step to great fortune will be to verify that your neighbor isn't home on the day of delivery. If the money doesn't arrive as scheduled, you'll have to find a new investment scheme. However, if it does arrive, you owe me big time.

Investment Seminars: A Few Tips

Each year, investment conferences are met with great anticipation. It's here you get to mingle with the "Who's Who" on Wall Street and with other junior gurus still in the midst of establishing their credentials. You may even run into famous financial authors with great ideas that don't work. Expect to be wooed and surprised.

The menu of keynote speakers frequently includes ex-politicians, ex-actors, and retired generals with no meaningful investment experience

---

*Exception: It's OK to give them your investment broker's phone number.

to speak of. Naturally, this group attracts immense curiosity. What will they say about the market this time, even though they've never ever discussed the market before?

The greatest part about investment seminars is the free giveaways. I like the complimentary pens, but the canvas bags are good, too. After you sustain large losses from the advice given, the bag will conveniently hold your personal belongings for when your spouse or next of kin evicts you from the house. If you're especially fortunate, you may even score a coffee mug from investment firms that won't exist in ten years. This corporate paraphernalia can become extremely valuable, especially on eBay. I'm still trying to get my hands on a Lehman Brothers beach towel.

Group Therapy

Investment clubs are a type of group therapy where one or more hopeful individuals pool their money together with the general aim of converting a few thousand dollars into millions, and, if all goes well, billions. Each of these members will contribute investment research and ideas to the rest of the group. After many days and weeks of debating, nobody listens to each other and, shortly thereafter, market orders are placed.

Club meetings offer an excellent opportunity to expand a person's waistline with cookies, donuts, ice cream, and cake. In certain places, particularly Central Illinois, this type of diet is considered the breakfast of champions. Sometimes these sugar binges will cause members to overstate the club's actual investment returns. Other times, nobody notices.

What to Do When Pop Goes the Weasel

What should you do if your investment account is bleeding losses? One immediate choice is to double or triple down on your losers and to pray they become winners. This particular course requires more play money, strong conviction, and an Evel Knievel motorcycle helmet. While this precise methodology has no formal name, I call it the "All-or-Nothing Shot."

Another technique for dealing with whale-sized losses is denial. In this respect, you have two more choices. First, you can flatly deny the existence of all market losses and treat them as a state of mind. Or, second, you can admit to owning losers but deny you actually authorized their purchase. Before taking this second route, make sure you can secure a good scapegoat, preferably a financial advisor or someone else who looks guilty.

The final method for handling losses is tremendously popular. It's called the "Wait-and-See Plan," and as its name indicates, not much work is required here—just lots of waiting. As such, I strongly advise against killing time by opening monthly statements, logging onto your online account, or tuning into any financial news. Having an upset stomach while you wait and see is not fun.

Ultimately, the decision to cut your losses is not always as straightforward as it should be.

I defer to a real life story about a widow whose portfolio of utility stocks was behaving like the biotech sector. Additionally, her trusty dividends had played a Houdini vanishing act. One particular utility had grown from a small problem into a big one. "My stock has fallen 97 percent. What shall I do?" she lamented. After analyzing her account statement, I told her, "If a 100 percent loss was your original goal, keep the stock." About ten seconds later, she invited me to leave. I don't know what her final decision was, but I assume she kept the stock.

Understanding Misunderstandings

I think customers and their financial advisors suffer from the same communication problems as parents and teenagers. The terminology used by each group is similar but with a completely different meaning and purpose. As a result, misunderstandings between the two groups happen all the time.

Take, for example, a simple miscommunication that needs no lawsuit or criminal investigation but maybe could use an arbitration hearing or two. An advisor honestly believes he sold the customer a mutual fund that invests in Estonia. Yet the customer honestly believes he bought a fund that invests in a different country. Neither party can agree on the actual transaction that took place. Who's right?

Before I tell you the answer, let me share with you a true story. It's about a 72-year-old man with a decent monthly pension. One day he surprised everyone by marrying a hot and wild cowgirl nearly half his age. Unbeknownst to both, their marriage turned out to be a slight misunderstanding. She married him for his pension; he married her for love.

Now back to the customer, the advisor, and their little misunderstanding. Here's what really happened: The customer tried to buy a mutual fund with market exposure to Spensonia but instead wound up with Estonia.* Next time, the customer needs to listen with ears instead of eyes.

Filing a Customer Complaint

The number of customer complaints about Wall Street over the past few years has been rising. Thankfully, most of these complaints have been resolved by giving away complimentary theatre tickets.

Other complaints are handled through a process called arbitration. How does it work? Someone known as an arbitrator (not arbitrageur) hears both sides of the dispute and then makes a decision. At best, the arbitrator will rule in your favor. At worst, the arbitrator will side with

---

*Slot machine players do this all the time. How do you think money keeps winding up in the wrong machines?

your adversary and wave your right to reverse the decision through litigation. Needless to say, arbitration is considerably less profitable than arbitrage. Perhaps this is the reason the former has been called the poor man's version of justice.

Class action lawsuits are another way of dealing with customer disputes. Should you decide to pursue this method, you will need a creative legal counsel and a gullible jury. (No I won't be your witness, but I hope you win.) One caveat: It is doubtful this technique will result in a capital gain for anybody other than your lawyer.

What's the best course of action for the customer—arbitration or litigation? Generally, I support whatever step or series of steps that fully restores legitimate victims to their original status while simultaneously paying attorneys the least amount.

Joining the Club

By now, all the prerequisites for becoming a Wall Street man or woman should be clear: a healthy imagination, a good long stubborn streak, and plenty of moxie. A strong back is also recommended, but no spine is required. Interestingly, many of Wall Street's best customers have these same characteristics, which opens up a brave new world of dreams beyond the ones they've already been sold.

For those of you contemplating a role change from customer to a Wall Street career, I send you my deepest condolences. You will get no such sympathy from hostile regulators, tyrannical supervisors, or ungrateful customers.

To help you along, I designed an exam to best determine where you should work. After you answer these questions, you will be given a suitable job fit. From there, it will be your chief responsibility to do everything in your power to avoid screwing up things any more than they're already screwed up.

1) *Non-farm payrolls were just released five seconds ago and the numbers look horrible. Should you sell everything?*

   A "yes" response to a single indicator, no matter how crucial you think it to be, points to a short and unsuccessful career as a trader. On the other hand, if your immediate reaction to the horrific payroll figures was to back up the truck and buy, then a career as a securities salesperson awaits you.

2) *Is it ever possible for one plus one to equal three, even for a brief moment, like during extreme market conditions?*

   Anyone who answers "yes" to this question is a prime candidate for an economist, a philosopher, or a hedge fund manager. If "no" is your response, I suggest you look into becoming an elementary school math teacher.

3) *There exists a certain company that is insanely profitable with an unfair competitive advantage and is in no need of any further financial or capital assistance. Should it be dismantled to create more value?*

   If "yes" is your very first thought, then a career in investment banking is your best choice. If your response is an affirmative "no," it's probably because you're the old grouch running the company.

4) *There exists a perfectly worthless company with an equally worthless management team whose stock price has cratered from $86 per share to under $7. Should the stock still be rated a "buy?"*

   Whoever answers "yes" to this question is immediately qualified as a securities analyst. It probably won't do you much good, but start studying for your CFA exam. Anyone who answered "no" should have shorted the above mentioned stock when it was at $86, not $7. You big dummy!

The customer's mind.

5) *The quarterly earnings of Corporation XYZ have beaten analysts' estimates by a penny for 56 straight quarters. Is that normal?*

Someone who believes this sort of fishy achievement is completely normal should work as a chief financial officer or corporate auditor. Anyone who denies the truth of this amazing feat should go into forensic accounting or securities regulation.

6) *Over the past 30 years, brainless index funds have outperformed 95 percent of mutual fund managers. Can you accurately guess which fund managers will outperform index funds over the next 30 years?*

Those who answer "yes" to this question have a promising career as a fund analyst or mutual fund salesperson waiting for them. On the other hand, if you believe 30 years of historical data are inconclusive and more information is needed, you should become a rocket scientist, a chemical engineer, or a university professor.

7) *Who made all of these ridiculous profits and how can we sue them? (Alternate question: Who made all of these ridiculous profits and how can we defend them?)*

If you asked either of the above questions, a bright career in the legal profession awaits you. Sue until they're blue! Defend until the end! On the other hand, if you believe these ridiculous profits were illegally acquired, you're well on your way to becoming a federal prosecutor, a mystery writer, or an attorney general.

The Customer's Mind

Maybe I've made it seem like being a customer is not fun. After taking market averages into account over a period of years, I can assure you, it is not. Financially speaking, it is dreadful to be a customer, and there is plenty of data that shows this statement to be true.

Yet, we cannot assume all customers necessarily exist solely to make a buck. Some just want a cheap thrill, others want fodder for dinner conversation, and others just want revenge. Will there ever be a perfect investment plan that matches all the psychotic phases of a customer's mind? I doubt it, but this lack will never prevent the investment profession from trying to find one.

I do not want the reader to mistakenly think all customers are haplessly misinformed or even dumb. There are plenty of customers, for instance, who have a better head for investing than the financial counselors they employ. Other customers have wizened up by switching their investment goal from getting rich to breaking even.

Even the brightest customer's mind is a fragile enigma that plays tricks on him. At any given time, it directs him to do the precise opposite of what he should be doing—like buying when he should be selling and selling when he should be buying or doing something when he should be doing nothing. And, at other inopportune moments, the customer's mind shouts totally unrelated things like, "Mow the lawn," "Pick up the kids," and "Call Mary."

Chapter 4
News, Views and Zoos

The origin of the media has been an epic struggle between fact and fiction, favoritism and fairness. Key events in this history were the invention of radio, television, the Internet, and the bullhorn. Behind this façade, as with most things in the business world, is a very large insurance policy with liability coverage for mistakes. And behind that big insurance policy is a big commission check being paid to one happy insurance agent.

Beyond these superficial layers are other superficial layers built upon an infinite number of other superficial layers. Let's analyze this bizarre state of emptiness together.

Fewer than ten seconds of tire kicking unveils an incredible find: The term "media" contains the word "me" just before "dia." In Spanish "*día*" means "day." Therefore, the word "med*ía*" literally translates as "me first today." Put another way, the media offers us a good case study in the narcissistic nature of *Homo sapiens*. To confirm this idea, we should probably examine a real life example.

Antics, Semantics, and Electronic Farms

An entire media subculture called "content farms" is waiting for you to click onto their phony news headlines. How do they operate? They begin by employing a large body of freelance writers to produce an even larger body of Website articles, video, and other unnecessary financial content.

Their goal is not to inform you but to create a Mecca of electronic clutter in order to increase their chances of being recognized by Internet search engines.

To accomplish this irritable mission, "content farms" make liberal use of repetitive sentences with one set of hyperlinked words after the next. I will perform a brief demonstration to show you what I mean.

> *Are you worried that* <u>*stocks*</u> *are headed for a major* <u>*stock market*</u> *fall? You're not alone,* <u>*stock investor*</u>. *But you can buy* <u>*stocks*</u> *cheap when the* <u>*stock market*</u> *goes down,* <u>*stock investor*</u>. <u>*Airline stocks*</u> *sell airline tickets, and to get cheap* <u>*hot deals*</u> *on travel tickets* <u>*click here,*</u> <u>*here*</u> *and* <u>*here*</u>. *The* <u>*stock market*</u> *is a vast marketplace and don't miss cheap hot deals on* <u>*airline tickets*</u> *anytime day or night, just like* <u>*stocks*</u>.

As you can see from this example, the "content farm" begins with a seductive introduction about the stock market and finishes with a cheap sales pitch to buy airline tickets. And the reader ends up with Plenty O' Nuttin'.

J(our)nal(ism) 101

There's more to journalism than what comes from "content farms" or from what a teleprompter tells a reporter to say; but it's not much more than the words produced by the Ctrl C and Ctrl V buttons on a computer keyboard that can copy and paste long paragraphs zippy fast. Copy and paste have become the very backbone of journalistic innovation over the past century—and if not—then at least over the past 25 years.

In either case, the word "journalism" deconstructed to its naked core leaves us with "our ism," which denotes a distinct set of beliefs, doctrine, myth, or theory that guides a group of people. Expressed another way, journalism reflects the hunches and ideologies of the individuals or organizations behind it.

News Я Us

I know this is an impossible definition for the typical media person to accept, so I'll prove it by loosely interpreting financial headlines grabbed straight from the horse's mouth.

"Billionaire Investor Makes Big Bet on Banks"

From this headline we learn a few things. The first great discovery we make is that there is still one remaining billionaire investor somewhere in the world. We next learn that this particular gent has a keen fancy for banks. Lastly, we learn that he likes to make "big bets," which no doubt answers the question of how he made his billions. It also explains how he will lose his billions. This event, I'm convinced, will be the reporter's next story.

"Quarterly Earnings Rise 2 Percent"

This is probably one of the most common reoccurring headlines you are bound to encounter; therefore, it is vital for you to learn about its insignificance. From this vague headline we discover that during one particular three-month period corporate earnings actually existed. Office party anyone? The only thing worse than quarterly earnings increasing by a paltry two percent is earnings that fall by a whopping two percent. After this headline has been published, the media will spend its subsequent days and weeks suffocating us with next quarter's earnings estimates, revisions, and re-statements.

"Does Good News Mean Bad News?"

This cutely asinine headline was crafted not by a journalist but by a securities analyst with a CFA designation. In most other clubs, his membership would have been permanently revoked for defamation to human intelligence. Moreover, not only is this particular analyst confused about the difference between good and bad, but he also suffers from a spatial disorder and can't distinguish between up and down.

"Now Hiring!"

This is not an actual headline but something I made up in order to illustrate a point: Don't believe everything you read.

"Market Bounces off Key Levels"

Finally, an interesting headline! But, unfortunately, the article was terrible. On a positive note, the journalist made his deadline.

"Why Did the Market Go Up?"

In this particular article the financial journalist explained: "It was a classic bull market rally that broke a temporary intermediate trading range with a sharp positive uptrend on surging trading volume after months of complacent consolidation." A shorter and probably better explanation of what really happened is something a chart reader once told me: "The market has legs but no brains."

"Is the United States the Next Greece?"

There is nothing correct about this particular headline. Besides being geographically inaccurate, it is structurally wrong, journalistically wrong, and anatomically wrong. Man can never be woman and woman can never be man. Furthermore, it is economically offensive to compare a nation of Big Macs to a nation of tzatziki. What is false to begin with cannot be made into truth, no matter how hard a journalist tries. Let it be known everywhere: The U.S. can never be Greece and Greece can never be the U.S. Just survey any *real* American or Greek and you'll see what I mean.

"News CEO Murdoch Compensation Drops to $18 Million"

From this dramatic title, we learn that an $18 million paycheck is "a drop." Ninety-nine percent of the world's population would be ecstatic to receive this sort of compensatory punishment, otherwise known as "a drop." And if $18 million is "a drop," just imagine what a $17 million paycheck would represent! Are there any words to describe such revolting inhumanity?

To help the poor journalist who wrote this despicable headline, I've reconstructed a new one: *"News CEO Gets Massacred with $18 Million Paycheck."* How does that sound for an attention grabber?

The "Smart Money"

People within the media make regular references to "smart money." They say, "The 'smart money' is buying or selling this or that." Therefore, it is with profound curiosity that we make the following inquiry: Just who is the "smart money?" Before we can find the answer, we must first determine what the "smart money" has been doing.

In the late 1960s, the "smart money" was accumulating nifty-fifty stocks. After several failed attempts at achieving riches and glory, the 1973-74 bear market thoroughly decimated the nifty-fifty concept. Today it simply goes by the "iffy-fifty."

After a few short years of hibernation, the "smart money" began piling into gold. And just as gold was touching all-time highs in the early 1980s, the "smart money" was buying. For the next two decades gold was proven to be dead money for the "smart money."

Just as it was believed the "smart money" had forever vanished in almost the same way as the saber-tooth tiger, it miraculously reappeared. During the mid to late 1980s, the "smart money" had turned to insider trading. After an abrupt, but profitable, orgy, the "smart money" went to jail. But all was not lost.

The 1990s ushered in a new era unlike any other for the "smart money." It hit the jackpot by investing in profitless technology stocks with sky-high valuations. Venture capital and IPOs were the rage. Suddenly out of nowhere, the 2000-02 bear market ate the "smart money," taking roughly $5 trillion with it.

We never learn the identity of the "smart money"
until its far too late.

After a brief hiatus from going broke, the "smart money" decided it was time to load up on real estate. Instead of learning from its previous misses in nifty-fifty stocks, gold, insider trading, and technology stocks, the "smart money"—true to its history of stubbornness—refused to call it quits. Beginning somewhere around 2003, the "smart money" devoured real estate. "God isn't making any more land" was the general consensus. Shortly thereafter, real estate devoured the "smart money," leaving behind lots of vacant homes, condominiums, and office buildings.

But that's not all. The really really "smart money" was simultaneously investing in credit swaps, collateralized mortgage debt and other complicated financial paraphernalia. Why? Because it was the "smart thing" to do. And the experiment worked well until everything began to unwind like a yo-yo. Predictably, the "smart money" was there to unwind with it.

Soon after, it was revealed the "smart money" had invested ungodly sums in private investment funds with fictitious performance. The final results followed the same general trend as the other failed experiments, but with slightly more pomp and circumstance.

As you see, the historical track record for the "smart money" is difficult to express in numbers, so I'll try with words: It falls somewhere between asinine and dumb.

Tops and Bottoms

I misspoke earlier when I said the only journalistic innovations over the past century were teleprompters and the copy and paste buttons on a computer keyboard. That was wrong. Actually, there's another major breakthrough I failed to mention—news tickers.

On financial broadcasts the news ticker is located at bottom of the television screen. (Some news tickers can be seen on the front of office buildings or at public airports, but this is only because they have yet to be ticketed for vandalism.) The main purpose of news tickers is to re-repeat what the anchor person just said. So if you missed the babble the first three times, you can read it again on the ticker several more times.

News tickers serve another useful purpose: They hide the unsightly lower half of the people on the screen. Double bottoms, as any technical analyst would agree, are just plain ugly.

Another ticker, but with stock market quotes, is provided for your viewing enjoyment. This particular ticker device has a 20 minute delay on all stock quotes, which means if Starbucks or another stock you own is trading sharply lower, please give it another 18 or 19 minutes to go back up.

In recent years, laboratory scientists have seen promising results using news tickers on rats. Aside from amnesia and 98 percent brain tissue loss, there are no other side effects.

Despite the enormous advances in tickerization, most financial programs have been reduced to timeless (not timely) investment advice, such as, but not limited to, "Mamma doin' fine," "Boo-yah!" and "Are you ready Skee-daddy?"

Prophesying Profits

One clever media establishment dubbed itself as the "Profit Prophet"—a colorful wordplay that I wish I could have coined first, but rascal copywriters beat me to it.

The basic idea or at least the premise is that you subscribe to their financial publication, they proceed to prophesy, and the trees in your backyard start growing money. The more followers the prophets get, the more profits everyone is supposed to make. I love it!

I would like to make a friendly suggestion to the Profit Prophets: Do not limit your clever work to single homonyms. As they say in the franchise business: "Expand." Please bear in mind this is a little business advice coming from a journalistic novice.

For your convenience, I have compiled a short list of five-star rated homonyms along with a bonus list of words that rhyme and similar looking words. In each case, I highly recommend their liberal usage.

Homonyms	Words that Rhyme	Similar Looking Words
Bare/Bear	Analyze/Fantasize	Alpha/Alfalfa
Bore/Boar	Asbestos/Prospectus	Buffett/Buffet
Buy/Bye	Babble/Scrabble™	Bride/Bribe
Corps/Corpse	Banking/Skanking	Contract/Cataract
Cents/Sense	Big Board/Slumlord	Cyclical/Cynical
Heiress/Eris	Chart/Fart	Ethnics/Ethics
Leased/Least	Cheery/Theory	Finance/Fiancée
Lone/Loan	Censor/Sensor	Führer/Furor
Night/Knight	Editor/Predator	Investigator/Instigator
Principal/Principle	Fees/Fleas	Lair/Liar
Prose/Pros	Fibonacci/Liberace	Message/Massage
Racket/Racquet	Invest/Molest	Morality/Mortality
Right/Write	Payroll/Play-Doh	Retired/Retarded
Sole/Soul	Publish/Rubbish	Risky/Risqué
Sweet/Suite	Reform/Deform	Speculator/Spectator
Traitor/Trader	Thesis/Feces	Taxes/Texas

While the media's belated entry into predicting the future has given us more opinions to sift through, the final results look pretty familiar. As Paul Samuelson observed, "Wall Street indexes predicted nine out of the last five recessions." If that's true, and we have no reason to believe it's not, then reporters have accurately predicted eighteen out of the past ten recessions.

"Top Stories"

All broadcasts begin with "top stories," which are hopefully long enough to take the audience to commercial break. On busy days, "top stories" can carry a news network well into the evening and sometimes into the following days, weeks, and decades. On very slow days, the audience is tormented with yesterday's news, commercial breaks, and more commercial breaks.

I think most media news rooms are a remarkable likeness to bar rooms across America where the patrons aim for a real good buzz and nothing more. On occasions when a "top story" can't be located, reporters will usually head for the airport to see if the waiting lines have gotten longer. "Has the gridlock worsened?" they ask. Of course it has. Your news satellite truck is blocking traffic, Sherlock. Meanwhile, the contest for the big story never subsides, even when none exists.

Certain media establishments have carved out distinguished businesses for themselves by republishing data that was formerly scribbled on bathroom walls at the Capital Grille.

Here's an example of lists you are likely to see:

- 50 Best Stocks
- 100 Best Mutual Funds
- Best Brokerage Analysts
- Most Expensive Zip Codes
- Highest Paid CEOs
- Top Retirement Destinations
- The World's Most Admired Companies
- The World's Top Billionaires

What do I think about these types of lists? As a rule of thumb, you should not make any life or death investment decisions based upon them, not unless dying is of no objection.

Building a Good List

In my attempt to gain journalistic acclaim (I will take national or local, too, if available), I have assembled my own unique list that contains the best corporate executives over the past 25 years. My list was constructed to report the facts without fear and without favor.

Best Corporate Executives*

1) Albert J. Dunlap, Sunbeam

2) Angelo R. Mozilo, Countrywide Financial

3) Bernard Ebbers, MCI Worldcom

4) Charles O. Prince, Citigroup

5) Dennis Kozlowski, Tyco International

6) Gary Pruitt, McClatchy Co.

7) Gary Winnick, Global Crossing

8) John Rigas, Adelphia

9) John Thain, Merrill Lynch

10) Kenneth Lay, Enron

11) Richard "Dick" Fuld, Lehman Brothers

12) Tony Hayward, BP

---

*Executives are not necessarily listed in order of importance or by prison cell block number.

My Second Attempt

If you did not enjoy my first attempt at list building, please give me another chance. You may be impressed to know that I have simultaneously constructed another list of the worst corporate executives over the past 25 years. This time, I promise not to let you down.

It should be noted that the same standards of accuracy, fairness, and authority apply to this second list, just as they did with the first. Lastly, the author has never had, nor does he currently have, a financial relationship with the executives on either list, nor does he desire any.

Worst Corporate Executives

1) Albert J. Dunlap, Sunbeam

2) Angelo R. Mozilo, Countrywide Financial

3) Bernard Ebbers, MCI Worldcom

4) Charles O. Prince, Citigroup

5) Dennis Kozlowski, Tyco International

6) Gary Pruitt, McClatchy Co.

7) Gary Winnick, Global Crossing

8) John Rigas, Adelphia

9) John Thain, Merrill Lynch

10) Kenneth Lay, Enron

11) Richard "Dick" Fuld, Lehman Brothers

12) Tony Hayward, BP

If after carefully comparing the names on both lists you've noticed they are exactly the same, not only would you be correct, but you are a lot harder to fool than I thought. You will also observe that each list contains two Garys and two Johns, so be very careful about using these names for children or household pets.

Naturally, both lists reflect my relentless commitment to journalistic objectivity.

Bow Ties and Sound Bites

The financial guests who visit established media forums, particular cable networks, are worth a brief gander. Is it puzzling to you why the same weirdos get all the air-time? It is simply because straight-laced visitors are bad for ratings. On the other hand, the "let's give them a good sound bite" guests are wonderful. Whenever there are two sides to an issue, they take five positions. Like a half-naked street performer, they generate loads of curiosity, which translates into loads of stunned viewers.

Out of a hundred guests there will always be one or two who wear a bow tie to remind everybody of the good old days back in the 1800s. I won't comment about their financial opinions, but investing in a full-length mirror isn't likely to be one of their recommendations.

The Blog Fog

Financial blogs and similar destinations are an ideal place to read nobody's opinion about everything. For instance, if you want to know if the market for European corporate bonds is overvalued, an endless trove of opinions awaits you. For those of us who know absolutely nothing about European corporate bonds, your comments and insight are welcome, too.

Many bloggers purposely write rude articles with the general idea of offending as many people as possible. And usually they succeed. Other bloggers exist solely to attack the establishment. They're determined to destroy Wall Street's aristocratic elite, even though most of these individuals and institutions have already done a brilliant job at self-imploding.

One of the most persuasive cases for investing in stocks I have read was written by a blogger. The article quoted market prices on two technology stocks, along with GDP numbers, candlestick charts, and a brief update on the housing market. The blogger then concluded that, while not everything "smells like roses," the market is "always darkest before the dawn." Wisdom, if I have ever seen it! Though the blog piece contained all of the financial references needed to solidify an equity investing argument, less convincing was the author's biography, which stated:

I have over 9 ½ months of investing experience, and I work in the IT department at a large computer software company. I blog about stocks, computer software, and gourmet cooking. When I'm not blogging, I'm cooking.

Needless to say, I never bought any of the stocks recommended by this particular blogger, but her banana bread recipe was outstanding—I gave it an Aa1 rating.

In summary, blogging falls somewhere between traditional news reporting and zoo-keeping. It is citizen journalism without a clear view of who the citizens are. You could also say it is grassroots journalism with lots of grass, but no roots.

Investing alongside the Electronic Mobs

Social investment networks are Web based communities where members communicate with each other via the Internet.

The principal theory behind them is that people in large quantities will make informed and disciplined decisions together. LOL!

Should you become an especially proficient social networker, it should not take long before you have 500 million friends giving you 900 million investment recommendations. BFF! On the other hand, if you've never visited a social network, it is basically equivalent to the Beardstown Ladies but with people of all sexes and a few aliens tossed into the mix.

Therefore, I make it my duty to forewarn you about all exercises in "social intelligence." If you put faith in the ability of mobs to make rational investment decisions on your behalf, your money will likely go missing. Then again, if you are interested in socializing while you try to make some money on the side, you'll love social investment networks. Join today!

Finally, as it pertains to all online forums, here is one more valuable tip: Avoid interacting with people who have the following user names: "Alan Greenscum," "InternetQween," and "WarrenBuffoon." None of them have any worthwhile financial advice to give or news that's fit to print.

Street Cleaning

Some of us still get our daily financial news from an outdated device called a newspaper. Thus far, I have resisted overtures to cancel my daily delivery, but the pressure is mounting. One newspaper editor (now unemployed) said, "We don't get paid for what we print; we get paid for what we don't print." Today, they don't do much printing or paying.*

I remember the time, before the Information Age, when my newspaper's business section had over 3,000 daily stock quotes neatly listed on four pages. Today, this very paper has just 10 daily quotes on the same four pages, but three and one-half of them are filled with advertisements for bankruptcy attorneys and buildable swampland.

What should you do if you're still part of the dying newspaper generation? I suggest keeping your subscription, especially if you have a family pet. Your newspaper still serves a practical purpose, if not to educate and inform, then to keep the streets clean from unnecessary animal waste. Newspapers also work great at the bottom of a bird cage.

---

*Source: People familiar with the matter.

Additionally, here is a humanitarian reason to consider: By maintaining your newspaper subscription, you will give publicly traded media companies another quarter or two to invent better explanations of why their businesses are still viable.

Last, my oscillating confidence in the diseased newspaper business is confirmed by the sage advice of a private equity manager from Beverly Hills who plunked down a substantial sum on a faltering daily. "I'm a big believer in newspapers," he was quoted as saying. Interestingly, his quotation did not appear in any newspapers to speak of, but it was picked up by one or two blogs.

According to Me

To say the media is infatuated with Wall Street is putting it mildly. It's akin to saying that Romeo and Juliet liked each other, or that Hitler was a mean guy. For good reason, certain media establishments have decided to relocate their headquarters far away from Wall Street's corrupting influences to secluded places like New Jersey.

Of course, none of this information should ignore the sometimes rocky relationship between Wall Street and the media. During one national broadcast a reporter asked a well-to-do financier, "How does it feel to be a billionaire?" After explaining his appreciation for island life, the poor gent was subsequently never invited back.

I think it could be soundly argued that we have had a bear market in financial reporting since 1929. In those days, even though much of very little substance was said, at least it wasn't pasted in every conceivable crevice 24/7.

Despite these setbacks, financial news reporting has come a long way since the late 1990s, when interviewing billionaire schoolboys on the eve of a big IPO was considered Pulitzer Prize journalism. Today, the financial media still carries out many valuable services. They have alerted us, for instance, to the fact that that Illinois Tool Works is based in Illinois, the *New York Times* is located in New York, and Texas Instruments is headquartered in Texas. On the other hand, Northwest Airlines is *not* located in the Northwest, but in Eagan, MN. After several attempts to reach them, spokespersons for major media outlets declined to give a statement or didn't return calls seeking comment.

Corrections and Amplifications

On behalf of all media organizations everywhere, I'd like to make a few editorial corrections. Most of these mistakes are so obvious nobody has bothered to notice.

Take Bernard Madoff's extravagant investment scam, which is consistently mislabeled by the media. Calling the Immaculate Deception a "Ponzi Scheme" isn't just bad reporting—it is blasphemous. While it's true that Charles Ponzi was the originator of multi-level financial perversity, Burny* was the master. Therefore, classifying multi-billion dollar swindles as "Madoff schemes," and not something less, is good for humanity as well as journalism.

You will also find the media politely referring to Madoff's throng of duped souls as "investors." I'm not so sure they were ever "investors" any more than buyers of lottery tickets are "investors." And if we continue calling them "investors," that means we have to begin calling slot machine degenerates and craps players "investors" too. Do you see how one bad teaspoon of inaccurate reporting causes a tidal wave of confusion?

A Little Job Placement Test

As an appendix to this chapter, I would like to supply the reader with some clues as to which individuals should, and which should not, pursue a career in financial journalism. Your answer to these questions or

---

*To eliminate any hidden biases, the author has purposely altered Bernie's name to "Burny."

reaction to the situations presented will tell us where you should work. If you refuse to take this placement test, you automatically fail.

Test yourself on these questions:

What's your opinion of a Wall Street man who has won a billion dollars? (If you say he's a crook, consider getting a job as a documentary filmmaker. If you think he's a genius, definitely go into public relations, or try joining the Dallas Cowgirls. On the other hand, if you think he's an idiot, you should try interviewing him, because he just might say yes.)

How do you react when someone knocks at your neighbor's door? (If you run to the window to see who it is, make your way directly to the newsroom, because a desk with a window awaits you. If you don't have any neighbors on your block, submit your job application for a park ranger, or something similar that requires limited human contact.)

Last quarter's corporate earnings were horrible. Is it news? (Anyone with the uncontrollable urge to publicly brag about poor earnings is somebody truly special. You have a bright future working as either a paparazzi or as an undertaker. When can you start?)

You have an ugly pimple on your nose. Do you stay at home or go to work? (If you said, "Stay at home," you should become a babysitter, a blogger, or both. If you said, "Go to work," you should not become a journalist but rather a makeup artist.)

Do you want to write 5,000 word articles about all the wonderful ways people can invest their money? (If you answered "Yes," look into becoming a securities analyst. You could always go into financial journalism, too, but it won't pay as much money. If "No" is your response, well done! There are no job openings for you at this time, but as the Ministry of Information once recommended, "Keep calm and carry on.")

This adjourns our discussion of the media.

Chapter 5
Investment Funds—Trial and Error Investing

The general idea behind mutual fund investing seems like an attractive proposition: You hire a reputable fund company, they get you a capable manager, the money rolls in, and you retire with more than enough cash—or some variation to the dominant theme of you getting rich. But, as we've seen, our lofty expectations of mutual fund performance and the reality of what we've received are light-years apart. High on promise and low on delivery, the actual results have ranged from less than average to plain disastrous. Or as one baseball coach observed about his underachieving roster: "With an infield like that, a routine ground ball is obsolete."

The individual investor, according to his hereditary inclinations, is out to make a killing. He wants his hundreds to turn into thousands, his thousands into millions, his millions into billions, and his billions into—well, you know—trillions. Although he's vaguely familiar with how he will accomplish this, he'll gladly take nothing less than a 37 percent return on his money year in and year out.

But there's a minor problem: No matter how much time he spends studying the market, the charts or whatever else, none of it makes sense. He can't figure out how the price of oil, the level of short-term interest rates, or how Asian stocks are influencing his 304 shares of Intel. "I could be exercising at the gym, teaching my grandchild how to ride a bicycle, or watching the sunset," he says to himself in a frustrated huff. And he's right. So, he sells the Intel shares and opens a mutual fund account. The people in the fund company's marketing brochure look happy. Why can't he be the same?

On paper, putting money in a mutual fund is the right move. Fund managers have good educations, fast computers, research staffs, inside connections, and other enviable resources. Put another way, mutual fund managers have everything they need to succeed.* Even if they are half as good as their resumes say, paying them whatever price will be worth it.

The Pitch

When proposals to invest in a molecular cloning stock come to mutual fund managers, they don't have to accept somebody's fifth hand word for it as you and I do. They immediately send a team of PhDs to examine the company's clinical studies along with its laboratories. Another team of forensic accountants comb through the company's financial statements. They have someone else check into the demand for cloned cells. And for whatever other things they don't understand, there's a biotech analyst at the brokerage firm where the fund company clears its trades who does. On our best day, we'll never know one-tenth of what any of these people know about molecular science or the company.

If the idea of mutual fund investing is even a fraction of being as good as it appears, the average investor has no business buying individual stocks or anything else but mutual fund shares. To illustrate this point, let's use the following analogy: If it was very important to win a lawsuit, and you were allowed to hire David Boies or another attorney of equal stature for a reasonable sum to make arguments on your behalf, wouldn't you be an arrogant klutz to insist on representing yourself? It's obvious that Mr. Boies or someone in his likeness is superior to us in a courtroom, and his mere presence is proof enough. But what is true in law is unfortunately

---

*There I go again misusing the word "succeed." How many times does this make it?

The money that sticks to the ceiling is yours.
Everything else is ours.

not true in the investment business. Up until now, there has been spotty evidence that skill and competence in managing a portfolio of securities can be bought. And even if it can be purchased, it either costs too much or it's not available for hire.

The Pay

How much money do mutual fund managers make? Because it's none of our business, let's investigate.

Based on what has been made public, the pay scale for fund managers follows a sharp upward sloping graph that goes from tolerable to obscene, and at times, to scandalous. One Wall Street gent, after decades of receiving this type of paycheck, gushingly stated, "Having a mutual fund management company is like having a toll booth on the George Washington Bridge all for yourself." Ever since then, I've been trying to obtain a toll booth. As I understand it, toll booths aren't required to comply with any of the rules contained within the Investment Company Act of 1940. Just imagine!

One prominent equity fund manager vacuumed in a delicious $46 million paycheck in 2008—a dreadful year for stocks. During the good years, as it was explained to me, he received an annual salary of just one dollar, so he was playing catch-up. Presumably, he will continue playing catch-up until he finally stops falling behind. Although he was harshly criticized for his lack of sensitivity to the unfortunate plight of his investors, he still kept the money. In spite of angry protests, fund shareholders agreed to give him one more chance.

Disinterested Directors

After much legal bickering for and against everything, it was decided that mutual funds should have a board of directors. It was agreed that these directors, for a modest upper tax bracket salary, would take time out of their tennis schedules to protect the interests of fund investors.

Minus a scandal or three, fund directors have anonymously gone about their business. Can you personally name one—just one—mutual fund director, either dead or alive? Good. That's the way they want it.

Contrary to what has been written, being a mutual fund director is not all wine and roses. At times, for example, it's scotch and daisies. When things are a real mess, fund directors are forced to work overtime. But in most cases, they'll gladly oblige as long as they get triple overtime pay.

What are the requirements for being a mutual fund director?

The rule states: "At least 75 percent of a mutual fund's board of directors is required to be disinterested persons." Come to think of it, I believe we just bumped into the hitch: The mutual fund board room has too many *disinterested* people and not enough *interested* ones.

On one occasion rekindling the interest of fund directors was tried. During a decisive board meeting, a director raised his voice to the rest and proclaimed, "In the interest of fund shareholders, I want to be independent!" Within a matter of hours, the director was shipped to Singapore by the other board members. Thus far nobody has heard from him to see how he has been enjoying his independence, but there's a good chance he's fine, because Singapore has country clubs.

Homage to the Alphabet

The philosophical debate surrounding the merits of investing in mutual funds that have no sales charges (no-load) versus those that do have a sales charge (load funds) is a perpetual one. Boston Red Sox and New York Yankees fans suffer from a similar dispute about which city has the better baseball team. (As a pathetic Chicago Cubs fan, I think they both stink, but that's another matter.) Although no-load funds and load funds are worlds apart in the way they assess fees, they share a common bond—the alphabet.

The increasing number of mutual funds in both camps has been aided, in part, by an increasing number of share classes that are typically identified with an alphabetical letter. Funds can generally be purchased in the following alphabetical categories: A, B, C, D, E, F, R, T, V, U, and Z. (Feel free to add any letters I missed.) What's more, each of these separate share classes contains a different fee, a different yield, a different performance return, and a different ticker symbol. What a fantastic labyrinth of redundant choices! What is the real purpose behind the mutual fund alphabet soup? Is it to give customers more convenience, as marketers claim, or is it to compensate the pantheon of financial intermediaries within the food chain?

It doesn't seem that long ago when load mutual funds were offered in just two or three share classes. It was a sort of Golden Age period for the financial services industry because it relieved fund salespeople from explaining the maze of hypothetical outcomes with prospective clients.

I once attempted to explain this to a mutual fund customer who kept pestering me.

"Which mutual fund share class represents the best deal for the individual investor," he asked.

"Well," I said, "The correct answer is really a question of mortality."

"Come on DeLegge, you're full of it!" he snapped.

I responded, "Class A-shares carry an upfront sales load and all but guarantee a painful but rapid ending. On the other hand, class C-shares do well at delivering a prolonged hurtful demise. Finally, B-shares are a deathly experience somewhere in between A and C."

He glared at me in a bewildered state of astonishment, and we never spoke again.

The main point to be learned is that a very tiny percentage of alphabet-riddled mutual funds have defied the odds because beating market averages isn't something in their genetics. Like the 98-year old smoker, it's amazing that those funds are still even breathing; however, I don't think you should go out and immediately buy these funds any more than you should take up smoking.

When Money is No Object

Critically acclaimed hedge funds are a unique investment category that defies categorization. A hedge fund is a type of investment fund that is offered to professional or wealthy investors who meet certain minimum financial criteria. There are far too many hedge fund strategies for me to cite, and, even if I could, the world as we know it would not be ready to bear them. The only thing I can think of that outdoes the sheer number of hedge fund strategies is the sheer number of hedge funds themselves.

Each year in hedge fund investing, billions are won (for the managers) and billions are lost (for the clients). Of course, this result hardly dissuades hedge fund clients from rolling the dice. They have faith the size of a mustard bottle, which occasionally relocates mountain tops to places where they don't belong.

Why are hedge funds that invest in risky assets still marketed and sold under the premise of safety and risk reduction? I really don't know the answer, but knowledge of this fact should give the SEC a few thousand new leads. Maybe it's because the typical hedge fund manager, like Mother Goose, believes the safest place for a cradle is on a tree top. As such, I strongly advise you against having these individuals care for your children or anything else of irreplaceable value.

The traditional view of hedge funds is that they are alternative investments managed by super smart people whose trades help to create much-needed market efficiency. But from what I've seen, hedge funds are not so much an investment category as they are a religious experience.

Before a person can even begin to understand the complicated world of hedge funds, we need to first investigate their habits. Let's begin our venture into the hedge fund religion by reproducing a close approximation of the dialogue between a hedge fund salesperson and a prospective client:

Prospective Client: Is that a convertible Bentley?

Hedge Fund Salesperson: Sure is, hop inside.

Prospective Client: Where are we going?

Hedge Fund Salesperson: First we can grab lunch and then we can go to Monaco for the weekend. And if there's time, we can even watch Tiger Woods shoot a round or two. Do you like football?

Prospective Client: Monaco? Tiger Woods? Football? What about the fund?

Hedge Fund Salesperson: The fund is up 82 percent. It puts the S&P 500 to shame.

Prospective Client: 82 percent? How does it achieve such impressive returns?

Hedge Fund Salesperson: It's a go-anywhere fund—wherever there's opportunity, it goes.

Prospective Client: Wow, that's amazing. What about the manager? He looks kind of young.

Mutual Fund Salesperson: Don't let the baby face fool you. He graduated from Harvard University in 1964 and once managed a private investment fund with Rockefeller's third cousin.

Prospective Client: Rockefeller? Wasn't he a billionaire? What does the fund invest in?

Hedge Fund Salesperson: Mainly uncorrelated assets.

Prospective Client: Can I meet the fund manager?

Hedge Fund Salesperson: He's in Thailand searching for good values.

Prospective Client: Who are some of your fund's investors?

Hedge Fund Salesperson: A few professional athletes, a few Hollywood types, and five or ten billionaires. Did you ever see that movie *Jurassic Park*?

Prospective Client: What about the fees?

Hedge Fund Salesperson: Fees? What kind of question is that? Our hedge fund pays for itself!

Prospective Client: Do you own any?

Hedge Fund Salesperson: In about another week the fund is going to be closing to new investors, so there's not much time.

Prospective Client: I like Bentleys.

Hedge Fund Salesperson: Did you know that Monaco is a tax haven?

Prospective Client: This hedge fund looks like a really smart investment. Isn't Tiger Woods the most amazing golf player ever?

Hedge Fund Salesperson: See, I told you so.

Prospective Client: Thanks for the Super Bowl tickets. Who do I make the check payable to?

My Buy Recommendation List

It would be entirely misleading if I told you there weren't one or two truly great hedge funds. I have been brainwashed to automatically say that there are in fact several good ones. Who are they?

This exclusive group of funds is supervised by the best money managers on the planet who were educated at the finest institutions. (Not the ones with padded walls or electric fences.) These are the managers who know how to make insider trading look like outsider trading. They are the managers who know how to shake down a corporate board room like Joe Bananas, but without getting caught. They are the same individuals who, in their spare time, enjoy reading and learning about themselves in *Vanity Fair* magazine. Do you *really* want to know who they are?

I'm displeased to announce that not one of these top hedge fund managers has paid me a consulting fee to be rated. Therefore, none of them have made it onto my buy list. Stingy grumps! Bothersome as that may be, there's a valuable lesson to be learned here: If you don't put people on your recommended list, they won't put you on theirs.

Fully Invested Elsewhere

As I was distracting you in previous chapters, I purposely avoided discussing the Internet orgy of the late 1990s. Isn't it fascinating that today's top authorities on the Internet boom and bust are the same people who, ten years ago, were like everyone else: its dupes? Usually, they talk and write about the subject in a condescending manner to insinuate that they were mere observers and not active participants in the madness. But not me! Frankly, I enjoyed the folly and wouldn't be the least bit bothered by a sequel.

The Internet boom was our era's version of absolute lunacy, quite comparable to other colossal misjudgments like surgery without anesthesia and smoking with no harmful side effects. Companies with no purposeful business, other than to become publicly traded entities, would go from $12 to $100 in a matter of minutes and then split shares like amoebas and repeat the entire process over and over. To their credit, a tiny population of elite money managers avoided the Internet meltdown all together, but it was only because they were fully invested in other places like Kodak, MCI Worldcom, and Enron.

In fairness, let's not forget that mutual funds have endured and survived through a difficult period known as the Lost Decade. And while many of these surviving funds would never win a beauty contest, there's no denying that live dogs are better than dead lions. So if fund managers behaved like berserk rodeo clowns—or something worse—during this forgettable period, look around and try to find people who conducted themselves better. Did you?

Cui Bono?

There's a hotly debated question about what is the better way for customers to pay for financial advice—fees or commissions. Rather than engaging in the argument of fees versus commissions, I propose that we analyze the matter from an entirely different angle.

For simplicity, I've categorized all mutual fund fees, charges, and commissions under one giant heading called "Haircut."* I've done this because practically everyone understands what a haircut is, except for Rastafarians. Even for those of us *without* hair, we can still appreciate this illustration because we probably know someone *with* hair. In a similar vein, whether you pay fees or commissions to a fund company, you understand that your hair (money) is getting cut (charged). The next question is which haircutting device is the best apparatus? Is it a chainsaw, a guillotine, a razor blade, a butter knife, or something else? And who's benefiting from all these haircuts? Is it the customers, or someone else?

As much as I like the haircut analogy to commissions and fees, it is lacking in at least one respect: Hair, when it's chopped off, grows back, but money doesn't.

In recent years, certain investment firms have promoted themselves as "fee-less entities." One establishment, whose identity I'm withholding to protect their stupidity, made its policy to charge absolutely no commissions or fees of any kind. For a while, the firm's clients were ecstatic, until it was later discovered that, after each market close, their money was tossed towards the ceiling and whatever stuck there was designated as client profits, while the rest was counted as fee income. Although the risk of gravity was never mentioned in the prospectus, it was a state of the art operation, with an emphasis on art.

---

*This same fee categorization method works quite well in other business fields like construction, healthcare, engineering, law, manufacturing, technology, etc.

High Hurdles

None of what we've discussed thus far negates the existence of top performing fund managers. On rare occasions someone somewhere beats the pants off of everything. But let's not confuse a hot streak with prudence or genius. How were those glorious returns obtained? Upon closer analysis, we discover the fund manager was leveraged to the hilt, or highly concentrated in just a handful of securities, or both. Another possibility is the manager's 100,000 share crapshoot on Capone Pasta Co. unexpectedly turned into the next Google.

In any event, pre-identifying top performers before they become that way is next to impossible. Furthermore, the management fees charged by most mutual fund families automatically erases the profitability of benefiting from whatever brief spurts in brilliance they have. *Sic transit gloria mundi!*

Cooking Lessons

Let's consider another set of financial arguments used by those who advise you to only invest with fund managers who "eat their own cooking." This is another way of saying to put your money with managers who invest their own money with themselves. The claim is made that managers' willingness to put their own money at risk alongside their shareholders is the best sign of credibility and integrity. (Maybe that's true, but it says nothing about whether they are delusional.) It is further asserted that managers who have a personal stake in their own funds show confidence in their investment ability. This claim sounds a great deal more logical than it really is. Think about it: If a portfolio of carefully selected holdings begins to sink like the Titanic, everyone's money sinks with it, including the manager's. When the ship is sinking, does knowing that the ship's captain is also sinking improve your odds of living happily ever after?

How would you like your haircut?
(Choose by checking applicable box.)

Likewise, it is presumed that a fund manager—by investing in his own fund—would avoid making counter productive investment decisions because it would damage his own finances. This, too, is wrong because demented fund managers who eat their own delicacies are a common occurrence. The main trouble is not whether they eat their own cooking—it is that their cooking stinks.

All of this reminds me of a knife throwing game between two men, with each serving as the other's target. One of the men objects to being the first volunteer, knowing that he will probably die if struck by his opponent's errant knife toss, but the other man assures him, "You have nothing to worry about sir. If you get hit, I lose."

A Short Lesson in Probabilities

What would happen, what absolutely *must* happen, if a group of people were competing against each other in a game of pure chance? To find out, let's go through a fascinating mathematical example. It will be up to the reader to determine whether mutual fund investing is a parallel exercise.

Let's start with a contest between 8,000 money managers. (This is almost equivalent to the same number of mutual funds currently available for purchase.) Each manager is given a coin, with heads representing a win, while tails is count as a loss. Anyone who flips tails is eliminated from the contest, while anyone who tosses heads is allowed to continue. Each of the managers is decorated with impressive business attire and required to have his mobile devices turned off so he can concentrate.

If the reader is at all mathematically predisposed, he should stop reading and work out in his head the final outcome; otherwise, the first coin toss ends with 4,000 winners and 4,000 losers. The second flip occurs, and half of the original 4,000 winners, by a stroke of good fortune, win again. We are now left with just 2,000 winners who are allowed another coin toss. The third flip eliminates half of that group, leaving us with just 1,000 winning managers. Onlookers are awestruck by the remaining winners who have won three straight games. Their "experience" has served them well. A fourth coin toss reduces our exclusive group of winning managers to 500, and the fifth toss cuts the number of winners to just 250. For their "hard work," these 250 winners are rewarded with a five minute break to study up on how to win the next round. However, the sixth game eliminates half of the previous round's winners, leaving us with just 125 jubilant players. After a few more flips, this group's size is cut to fewer than fifteen, and, by this time, word about their "talent" has begun to spread from Boston to Acme, Oklahoma. For their "prudent" flips, the remaining winners are given five stars and interviewed about their achievements. Eventually, there are fewer than five winners who have won a dozen consecutive coin flips. This super-exclusive group is designated as the experts who never lose and who receive open invitations from Congress and elsewhere to speak their minds.

I understand it is oddly absurd to equate mutual fund investing to a coin tossing game. It requires a certain amount of expertise to choose which securities a fund should own, right? The problem is figuring out how much more expertise is required. I certainly don't know, and I think those who say they do are bluffing.

Investing over the Long Run

Investing with a long-term view is sold as the panacea to whatever investment problems you face. More time is the magic potion for fixing a bear market, for repairing ill-timed investment moves, or otherwise healing a person's masochistic tendencies. As good as that may sound, is it really so? Let's put this theory to the test with a real life example.

Meet Jeanne Louise Calment. She was born in Arles, France, on February 21, 1875. By the time she was 90 years old, in 1965, she figured it was time to cash in and retire. So Calment agreed to sell her apartment to her lawyer Francois Raffray. For Raffray, who was just 47 years old, it was an ideal long-term investment and one that would surely be profitable. He agreed to pay Calment monthly installments until she died. Like 99.9 percent of long-term mutual fund investors, Raffray was already analyzing, projecting, and reanalyzing his unearned winnings, because time was on *his* side.

Ten years blew by, 1975 arrived and Calment was still alive. And Raffray was forced to keep paying her. His long-term investment had yet to pay off, but soon it would. Meanwhile, he kept analyzing, projecting, and reanalyzing his future gains. Eventually, the year 1985 arrived, and to everyone's great marvel (except Raffray's), Calment wasn't just alive, but she was doing all of the things that 110-year-old people aren't supposed to do. She was fencing, cooking, and bicycling. And Raffray kept paying. But soon, according to his long-term projections, he would be vindicated!

When another decade passed and 1995 arrived, Calment was still alive, defying mortality statistics and snubbing the grim reaper. Then the long-term investing game suddenly came to its screeching finality. Raffray died of cancer at age 77, leaving his widow with an unlucky inheritance: the responsibility of paying Calment another twenty months before her death on August 4, 1997.

Raffray's real life experience is a textbook example that no amount of long-term planning can compensate for an errant investment bought in the wrong year at the wrong price or from the wrong someone. Running into the incorrect long-term period or person can end badly. Then again, if you're fortunate to live long enough to the overripe age of 122, like Calment, you might have plenty of time to recover from your mistakes. But even so, I strongly caution you to be very careful about the long-term investment decisions made between ages 115 to 121.

Ultimately, long-term investing like *all* investing is fraught with uncertainty. Waiting a few decades for your investments to produce gains certainly puts the odds in your favor, but it hardly guarantees a pleasant outcome.

Beating the Market

Why not just invest everything in mutual funds that outperform? Unfortunately, this technique does not work very well, mainly because today's hot shots are tomorrow's turkeys. This unhappy rule of thumb is not limited to investments, but also applies to other fields like art, entertainment, politics, medicine, science, and sports. Regardless, mutual fund companies have not stopped bragging about their performance, even during a tailspin.

Toward the end of 2008, which was a horrible year for stocks, one manager boasted about his fund's performance. The S&P 500 declined by 38.5 percent, while his fund declined by just 32 percent. Since nobody bothered to recognize his achievement, I'd like to offer a much deserved hat tip: Congratulations sir; you beat the market.

The Expanding Universe and Some Odds

Three mutual fund categories we haven't discussed are Mongolian equity funds, dermatology/wound care funds, and target date retirement funds. Since none of these categories are hot performers right now, I don't imagine there's much interest in reading about them.

Despite the difficulty in helping fund investors reach financial utopia, Wall Street remains confident the slump is just a short-term blip. In the meantime, fee income is growing and the product development team is on a roll. The number of new funds being launched is infinitely expanding, just like the universe. Never before in history have there been so many wonderful investment opportunities that you and everyone else should probably avoid.

Finally, suppose you believe your money should be equally divided between stocks, bonds, and cash, and you ask me, "Do you think a reputable fund company could do a better job at buying and selling securities than I could do on my own?" My immediate answer would be yes, but with a caveat the size of King Kong. A professionally managed fund can probably do better than you, but a mixture of brainless index funds or ETFs held over a period of time can do even better. The statistical studies prove this to be true, and whatever numbers are lacking, Las Vegas oddsmakers will vouch for. Finally, to answer the question of whether or not any of it will outperform the cash in your right-hand pocket, I promise to have a definitive response for you in five or ten years.

Chapter 6
Advanced Strategies for Beginners

A Midwest traveler took a weekend road trip to get away from the city. It began as a pleasant excursion, but within a matter of hours and several cornfields later, he was lost. So he pulled into a gas station to get directions. "Where's Attica?" he asked. "It's near Indiana," replied the station's attendant. Frustrated and puzzled, the traveler insisted, "Where's Indiana?" The impatient attendant abruptly smirked, "It's near Attica."

The less than satisfactory directions received by this traveler motivated him to invest in a more sophisticated mapping system. Because of this incident, he no longer trusts gas station attendants. And while he has never yet crossed through Attica, he has been close.

Let's consider a few advanced investment strategies meant for beginners or otherwise lost passengers.

Scrambled Eggs

Diversification is the art of holding different assets within an investment portfolio. Instead of owning one stock or bond, for example, you would own many. Should any number of those stocks and bonds become totally worthless, you'd still own the others, so theoretically you're still in the game.

Diversifying one's risk dates back to ancient times. During the Stone Age, the natives diversified by having enough children to make a football league. Today, their offspring have graduated to diversifying with securities.

I was once invited to learn about this strategy firsthand while working as a trainee under the supervision of a veteran broker. It was my opportunity to finally unearth sales secrets from the heavy hitters. We ate dinner at a swanky joint with a client who had amassed a large portfolio in just a handful of stocks.

"How are my investments doing?" asked the customer.

"OK, but your portfolio is missing a few things," said the broker.

"How am I performing?" insisted the customer.

Ignoring the question, the broker continued, "If we divide your investments into 26 pieces instead of just four, you'll have more money."

By that time, the check for dinner had arrived, and it was time to go.

The worried customer was immediately sold professionally-managed rubber cement futures to defend against inflation.

I don't recall how bad inflation got, but the client had momentarily achieved financial peace of mind. He now owned everything.

LEVERAGE

Although it looks like some sort of eye examination, the word above this sentence is "leverage" with its letters fashioned to illustrate just how dangerously fun leverage can be when written on a screen or a piece of paper. In practice, it is analogous to a jalapeño pepper that can either complement your favorite meal or turn your tongue into a cooked hamburger patty.

The concept of leverage is easily applied to trading with a margin account. We assume it's a wise and a profitable endeavor to spend $2,000, buying 100 shares of Pfizer at $20. But what if we could buy 200 shares with the same $2,000? And suppose we could make it 400 or 500 shares

If we divide your investments into 26 pieces instead of just four, you'll have more money.

with the generosity of a broker who will lend us the money? Should we do it?

The answer is a flat no, and to learn why, I invite you to try it. Be sure to use money from your own stash, not grandma's, and report back to me how you made out. I doubt leverage will greatly improve your returns, but go ahead and give it a shot.

Despite my own personal apprehension towards leverage, I'm familiar with the arguments for it. What about the leveraged buyout kings? Didn't they make fortunes through the prudent use of leverage? And what about the small group of others who amassed great wealth during the credit bust with borrowed money?

Listen, you are nothing like them. They are calculated risk takers, disciplined, and well-informed. Actually, I don't know if any of that is true, but how else shall we describe psychotic daredevils without hurting anyone's feelings? Who knows, they could just as well have made their fortunes for the exact opposite reasons, which is precisely what I suspect.

Stock Ratings, Decoded

The exact interpretation of analyst stock ratings has created something of a quagmire. At various moments, like possibly right now, a buy rating really means sell, and a sell rating really means buy. On other occasions, a downgrade is just a disguised upgrade. And, a hold rating is not really a hold but a sell recommendation with subtle overtones. Who are the people behind this perpetual madness? Let's investigate further.

The equity analyst is a sight to behold. His professional experience at recommending stocks begins with a fast buy recommendation on shares of whatever. His pick hardly deserves to be rated as a "buy," but since everyone else is recommending stocks, he figures it wise to do the same.

In short order, his lone recommendation rises from $25 to $100.*
He is crowned as a genius, and people start to correctly pronounce his
impossible last name. A capable public relations department will get him
a few TV appearances to discuss his views on the market. People are
awestruck by his outlandish views. He's so wise!

Our analyst is further emboldened by the stock's sharp upward
trajectory, so, hoping to repeat his sole success,** he proceeds to aggressively
add other stocks to his firm's buy list. His picks go straight to the moon.

In enough time, our analyst loses his mojo. His wonder list of
recommended stocks that briefly visited the moon has taken a detour to
the basement. Then he turns gun-shy. Instead of being brave and direct,
he becomes ambiguous. Here's a sample of market advice I poached from
a Wall Street equity report that he is destined to give:

> *Today's action in the S&P 500 is worrisome because it wasn't
> supposed to happen until tomorrow. The index registered a marginal
> decline on brisk trading volume, which could be the sign of a bear
> cloaked in bull's clothing. It wasn't necessarily a bloodbath, but two out
> of every three stocks closed lower, while six out of nine sectors remained
> stuck in neutral. This is a major setup for the possibility of a market
> transition from higher highs to lower lows, and prices are quite volatile.*

Now, if we took these words and put them to Calypso music, I'd
say there's an outside chance we might score a top 40 hit, which also
might be our best hope for converting the analysis into profits. Until
then, our analyst is reduced to a shadow of his former glory, and even
that is probably being too generous.

---

*We won't mention anything about his other stock picks or what they've done because "no
news is good news," as they say.

**There I go again, confusing the reader by misapplying the word "success." Cease and desist
already!

Finding the "Best" Investments

The notion of "best" investments deserves a closer look. If we conducted a survey of the "best" investments in history, we would find them to be a moving target that changes from one period to the next. Why? Because the "best" investments, in truth, are just the most popular—the most talked about, the most hyped, the most heavily traded, and, for that reason, the highest priced at that moment. It boils down to a choice of fashion, like zoot suits or Tutti Frutti hats. When beehive hairdos were in style, people thought "Nifty-fifty" stocks could be bought and held forever. When platform shoes were being worn, gold plated trinkets were the rage. To say that technology stocks were the investment *de jour* in the late 1990s is putting it mildly. And over the past few years, people have been snapping up government bonds and other financial instruments that yield close to zero percent. Scattered among these trends are other disparaging fashion movements that arrive just as fast as they leave— like auction rate securities, satellite radio stocks, business development companies, cancer ETFs, 130/30 funds, and century bonds.

The futility of selecting "best" investments was proven in an experiment of primates versus *Homo sapiens*, in which it was asserted that a blindfolded monkey throwing darts at a newspaper's financial pages could select a portfolio of stocks that could perform the same or slightly better than one carefully selected by the experts. The end results showed the monkey's stock portfolio did indeed hold up better in a declining market when compared to the expert-picked one. Because of these findings, an entire generation now invests just like primates. Those who haven't already switched their investment accounts to monkeys use the same dart-selection methods for picking stocks. "If a dart-throwing monkey can achieve respectable returns by guessing, why can't we?" they ask.

Tips on Insider Trading

Using non-public information that is material and trading on it is a crime called "insider trading." As has been demonstrated, the penalties for insider trading are very high, and the rewards for not getting caught are even higher.

Illegal insider trading would occur, for example, if a significant shareholder at Company A learned (before it became publicly known) that Company A will be acquired, and that shareholder bought shares in Company A ahead of the acquisition, knowing its share price would likely rise. Any profits made are illegal. There are numerous other intriguing variations of insider trading that my cranky legal department won't allow me to list.

What about the persuasive arguments in favor of making insider trading a lawful activity? Generally speaking, the individuals making these claims also want to legalize narcotics, prostitution rings, and organized crime. The other proponents of legalized insider trading were once kidnapped and now suffer from Stockholm syndrome.

While I personally don't agree with legalizing insider trading, I understand its basic premise, which is to give chaos a chance. Does that sound like something we should try? Doesn't the world already have an adequate sum of mayhem? Do we need insider trading to add more?

Day Trading as a Career

One of mankind's greatest shortcomings is that he wants what he cannot have. Every day he reminds himself about what he doesn't have, and, along the way, he forgets about the good things he possesses. This is the same way he treats his employment, if he has any. He's sick of the daily grind, so his big plan is to get ahead by beating the entire world at its own game. Whether he realizes it or not, the earliest seeds of becoming a day trader have been planted inside his deepest inner being, and escaping won't be easy.

A day trader looks at the physical work of a bricklayer or janitor with contempt because he knows there are faster ways to make a buck than laying bricks or sweeping dirt. A day trader's ambition comes from Wall Street's traders who win millions and sometimes billions within a matter of seconds by merely pressing the right buttons on a computer keyboard. The typical day trader—and there are none—is convinced that trading, like other lines of work, is a realistic career that anybody can do.

But here's the chief problem: The millions and billions of dollars disappear just as quickly using the same keyboard methodology described above. And when it happens, the investment firm can blame it on a bad quarter, a flash crash, a rogue trader, or whatever other plausible excuses shareholders and the media will buy. Winning back the missing money is magically accomplished through a huge bond sale or a secondary offering. In contrast, the average day trading citizen has no such conveniences. The money that is lost is gone.

I do not want to be misquoted as saying that all trading activity is a useless endeavor, because there are limited instances where it can serve a useful purpose.

Take Joe, for example, who works for ABC energy, a company in the oil and gas sector. He has been closely observing oil prices and has discovered that oil's future price is $110 per barrel, while current or spot prices are at $90. Even though oil prices could slip below $90, Joe decides to buy a mother lode of oil at the spot rate of $90 per barrel. He believes it's best to limit his company's risk by locking in oil at a fixed price. If oil happens to soar, he will have saved his company a lot of money. On the other hand, if oil falls below $90, Joe will look like a dunce. This dilemma raises a few proactive questions: Is Joe engaged in a worthwhile venture? Does the size of his trades help him, or anyone else, to know the future direction of oil prices? What's the difference between Joe and small-time day traders?

If you interview Joe, he will tell you that his trading activity allows his company to hedge against unexpected movements in oil. He will also tell you (if he's honest) that his knowledge about oil's future price is limited, regardless of the size of his trades.

The main thing to remember is that Joe is on the company payroll, so even if his trades lose money, he still gets paid. In contrast, self-financed day traders aren't so fortunate. But what if Joe loses a large chunk on bad trades and gets fired? Don't worry; he won't—at least not yet.

Despite my good faith efforts to steer you in the right direction, my advice has probably fallen on deaf ears. And so, to demonstrate the doubtful nature of day trading as a long-term profitable exercise (a career), I know of only one way to conclusively prove my point: Try it. Before you can learn to swim, you must first drown. Only then will you appreciate what I'm saying. There are certain things that can only be conveyed through real life experience. Touching a hot tea kettle is one of them, and day trading your investment account down to its last $6 is another.

Something for your Third Personality

Anybody with schizophrenic tendencies will enjoy bond investing. Gains in the value of your bonds are immediately offset by losses in the income of your bonds. Conversely, just as the income from your bonds begins to rise, their value subsequently falls.

The weird inverse relationship between bonds and interest rates is comparable to a contrarian investor, who is genetically disposed to do the opposite of everyone. According to theory, this sort of perpetual disagreement with the other side, besides destroying plenty of decent marriages and wonderful families, is supposed to produce large financial gains. Regrettably, whatever gains are made—if any—are frequently negated by the cost of divorce proceedings.

One of the best descriptions I ever heard about bonds was from a commodities analyst who stated, "Bonds are backwards."

The Exciting World of Penny Stocks

What if you could buy thousands and thousands of shares of stock in a company for just pennies? Would you be interested? Welcome to the exciting world of penny stocks.

As their name implies, penny stocks are publicly traded companies whose shares trade for just cents. Most of these stocks were formerly listed at the local penny arcade but have now been transferred to either the OTC-BB or Pink Sheets to reduce overhead. In some cases, penny stocks can trade for as high as $5 per share. Just imagine if you bought 10,000 shares of a three-cent stock and it soared to $5. Isn't that exciting? What if it went to $500 per share? Isn't that exciting?

This is just the beginning of your thrilling journey into the bold world of penny stocks. After your initial purchase, you will be assigned a stock promoter to tell you about once-in-a-lifetime investing opportunities several times a week. In addition, you will get three years' worth of press releases over the next six months.

If you really want to learn more about penny stocks, you should immediately drop this book and try buying some. Like hang gliding at 3,000 feet above sea level, mere words cannot express the experience. Within a matter of weeks or probably less you will be transformed from student into teacher. You may even lose some money along the way before noticing your odds of turning a profit at the penny arcade were better. And, in hindsight, that's not too exciting.

What Do the Charts Say?

I'm forced to cover the subject of technical analysis because I don't want to offend chartists any more than I already have.

Let's begin with the 200-day moving average, which has risen to prominence as a technical indicator. It says if stock prices are above their 200-day average, buy; but if stock prices are below that average, sell. Forget about whether this is a profitable way to buy or sell anything. Why does Wall Street use 200 days for the moving average and not some other time frame? I think it's mainly because the 47-day moving average doesn't sound as impressive, and, furthermore, nobody* uses it.

Based on my own personal experience, I'm wise enough to know that any considerable graph should automatically trigger a case of double vision. Unfortunately for me, all the profits I had were diverted to my optometrist.

In technical analysis you'll find that charting bonds on a 52-week graph is a considerably different experience than charting biotech stocks on a 52-week graph. In any event, I've come to the conclusion that all charting is akin to John Madden's analysis of a football game:

> *They were having a tough time getting past the 40, then, BOOM, they broke across midfield to the 30. Then, BANG, the defense got tough and drove 'em back to the 50. But the offense pushed through some stiff resistance and, WHAM, got back to the 30. Guys, this game could go either way.*

Never have I met chartists from Cancun to Bavaria who have failed to correctly predict a bear market or anything else of any kind. If it wasn't for the graph with the patterns of a Burberry scarf that cued them, then it was the one with the death cross. That's because the charts are always right—in retrospect.

---

*Your Aunt Lulu doesn't count.

*This particular chart accurately predicted
the last bear (and bull) market. It also doubles as an abstract
painting for your home or office.*

Crash Course in Derivatives

Like the words coming out of a tranvilaquist's mouth, derivatives are fairly easy to identify. If you've never seen one, smelled one, or heard one, you'd never know the difference. How big is the derivatives market? It's a multi-trillion dollar cesspool of unknowns.

Understanding the real inside story about the complex inner workings of derivatives is very similar to watching the two-toed sloth during mating season. At first sight, an untrained person cannot detect what's occurring. Everything is so slow, it's a blur. One must seek professional help to really "get it," and derivatives are the same.

Who knows more about derivatives than Wall Street? The Street's financial experts not only "get it" but they know how to spell the word "derivative" on the first try. Furthermore, they are the sort of striking damsels and gents with seven to nine digit incomes. If they don't know everything there is to know about derivatives, then who does?

Regrettably, getting hold of these experts for more insight about derivatives is not so easy—I tried. They're busy in meetings, they're traveling, they've got dinner plans, they're on sabbatical, or they're not allowed to talk to unimportant little dust mites like me.

As a result, I'm left no choice but to paraphrase what one Wall Street hotshot said as he was pondering the limitless possibilities of derivatives: "What if we created a 'thing' that has no purpose, that is absolutely conceptual and highly theoretical, and that nobody knows how to price?"

Please note the above explanation about derivatives came from a caviar person, which means we need to decode its true significance. Put another way, certain derivatives (more than we can count) are all potatoes and no meat. This tasteless conclusion seems to concur with Wall Street's insatiable lust for form over substance. Now do you understand?*

---

*See page 397 for more insight into derivatives.

Alternative Investments

There are many other exciting investment opportunities I have not yet mentioned. I was unable to categorize this next group of investments inside a Morningstar Style Box, so we'll just call them "alternative investments" and give ourselves a quadruple A-rating for fast thinking.

Here is a short list of alternative investments along with my current market outlook:

Art

Stay away from the kind of art that melts, sheds, or endangers your life. Diamond encrusted skulls are okay, as long as the skull isn't yours.

Baseball Cards

In fairness to today's ballplayers whose cards are worth next to nothing, are we absolutely sure Babe Ruth didn't use steroids? Maybe someone can exhume his body to find out.

Beanie Babies

When besides never have Beanie Babies ever been a good investment? And if they're so great, how come Ty Warner is the only billionaire because of them?

Concert and Sporting Event Tickets

There's definitely money to be made scalping tickets, but there's even more dough to be made scalping securities.

Emerging Market Bonds

If Sri Lanka defaults on its bonds, who do I contact, and which windows do I break? Since I don't trust them with their own money, why should I trust them with mine?

Sperm Banks

Sorry, FDIC insurance is not offered on deposits.

Private Equity

Forget about what this high sounding opportunity actually is. The mere mention of private equity at a cocktail party is bound to impress! It's worth at least a free round of drinks and hors d'oeuvres, don't you think? Send the bill to the partners and see what they say.

Tax Exempt Sewer Bonds

What's so stinky about tax free income? If you can't handle the credit risk, then get out of the sewer.

Condominiums in Las Vegas, Miami, or Phoenix

No comment.

Timeshares Anywhere

No comment.

Timeshares in Beautiful Hawaii

I *said* no comment.

Saving for Retirement

The 401(k) is one type of popular workplace retirement plan whose name was adopted by Congress because R2-D2, 600 SEL, and WD-40 were already trademarked.

Here is the essence of 401(k) plans: Employees volunteer to have their wages deducted and sent to a tax-deferred account with a diversified menu of investment choices they don't understand. The idea is to guess well and hope they end up with more money than they started with.

Faced with a bewildering array of investment funds to choose from, the typical worker with a 401(k) usually follows one of the following methods: 1) invests in the funds with the best historical performance; 2) invests equal amounts in all funds; 3) invests everything in the money market fund and decides on the rest later; 4) sticks with company stock; or, 5) invests nothing in the 401(k) plan at all.

The first approach ensures that the worker buys last year's hotshot camouflaged as this year's turkey. The second technique is democratic at best, and not much else. The third strategy sounds good on paper, but procrastination usually wins the race. The fourth method looks okay, unless the company becomes the next Woolworth's. And the fifth way is almost always the first choice for financial atheists, because they don't believe in the existence of markets or other bogus concepts like performance, interest rates, money, and the like.

What should you do if you're like the millions of Americans with a 401(k) plan that has been decimated? The secret to getting back on track is to save more money. You don't want to eat cat food when you're grandma's age, do you? Just think about it: Even if the stock market falls 25 percent, and you stash away an additional 25 percent on top of what you're already doing, you'll be 25 percent richer. Isn't that exciting? And if you can't save more money inside your 401(k) plan because you're already saving too much, the best solution is to save even more. Once you've taken these vital steps, the next course of action will be to make a solemn promise to never touch your 401(k) money for any reason whatsoever—not even when you're 83 years old and broke. You don't want to eat cat food when you're 94, do you?

In summary, 401(k) plans were invented as a last ditch effort to persuade the American public that their chances of investment success are still pretty good. Coincidently, poker tables and slot machines were invented for the same reason.

A Little Daydream

This seems like an opportune time to take a short break from our discussion and do some daydreaming.

Let's imagine for a moment that there is a secret way to completely avoid the risks of investing. All of your previous worries about losing money are now completely gone.

Let's further suppose that, in addition to completely avoiding the risks of investing, you could also miraculously evade the stock market's downward spikes. When everyone else is getting crushed, you're printing money. And, when everyone else is printing money, you're printing even more money. You're making money no matter what and without any risk! How are you enjoying our little daydream so far?

You furthermore discover that the secret to your success—besides your own self-brilliance—is a trading software package that can be obtained for just $79. The program has 100 percent accuracy all the time and tells you what you should be buying or selling along with the precise moments to execute your trades. You press a few buttons on your screen and ridiculous profits instantly follow.

Finally, let's presume all of these things allow you to compound money at a very high rate of return for decades. How does a 35 percent return over the next 56 years sound? Is that high enough, or should I upwardly adjust the figures to account for your acumen?

Now that I've embellished our little daydream to the point of ecstasy, I have some unfortunate news. None of these things—the investing without risk, the uninterrupted self-brilliance, the always correct trading software, or the instant profits—actually exist, because they're all giant fantasies.

Post-Daydream Reality

Let's say you want to make some money. You see an article on the Internet about a guy who has a $3.6 billion investment portfolio after starting with just $423. You want to try the same thing. So you hire a financial advisor, telling him about the guy in the article. "I want my portfolio to look like this," you say. But a few things happen.

First, your financial advisor only knows how to build investment portfolios with stuff approved by his compliance department, which includes, among other things, a long list of mutual funds and variable annuities you've never heard of. But he wants your business badly, so he works hard to convince you that fashioning your investments after the billionaire guy's portfolio is a bad idea. He tells you it'll never work because $423 isn't enough money to build the Taj Mahal. He also explains that it's the sort of portfolio that would never survive a tornado. But you refuse to listen, because $3.6 billion is a lot of money to walk away from.

Your next hurdle is to find a financial advisor who 1) knows how to convert $423 into $3.6 billion and 2) will agree to work on your behalf for minimum wage.

After many attempts you're unable to locate any such advisor, but you're still not giving up. So you scour the Internet—the article's original source—looking for clues. You gather information—lots of it. You come across the life story of Michael Milken and all of the Filthy Rich Ones. None of it makes any sense, so you re-read it, but this time with the assistance of a Morse code translator. You study it hard.

Then, by random chance, it occurs to you that $423 isn't enough money to invest in the same manner as a tycoon. Now if someone—anyone—who knows something would just help you.

Soon you're forced back into the daily distraction of life, and then, out of nowhere, your plan to become a self-made Wall Street-styled mogul is suspended. Your dog becomes deathly sick because it couldn't digest the Tonka truck that your kid fed it. So you rush the animal to the veterinarian. Seven hours later you get the bill. It's for $423. The seed investment for your $3.6 billion portfolio is blown to confetti. The heartbreaking part is that you never even invested a single dime.

Chapter 7
Earth, Wind and Taxes

Since we've already spent the better part of this book discussing various investment techniques that sound great but don't work, we might as well talk about another anguishing subject: Taxes.

The history of taxes is almost as old as the history of mankind. Around 5,000 years ago, Egyptian Pharaohs imposed a tax on cooking oil. Citizens were subsequently audited to make sure they were complying with the rules. If it was discovered they were using inadequate amounts of cooking oil or other cooking methods to bypass the usage of taxed oil, they were penalized. Although the Pharaohs are gone, taxes remain.

Today, the subject of taxes only comes up a few times a year, which is way too much for most of us. So if I've added to that frequency with this chapter, you can blame the IRS.

Taxpayers

Anybody who pays taxes automatically becomes a taxpayer. You are now entitled to a long list of wonderful advantages, such as having your taxes temporarily reduced after they've been permanently raised. To get even, some citizens have decided to permanently underpay their taxes. If you're one of them, you will be caught, prosecuted and jailed—allegedly. Until then, eat, drink and be merry.

Taxpayers are categorized into tax brackets that correspond to their level of income. Should you have a particularly high income, you are assigned a top tax bracket, unless you can prove you are poor. In contrast, should you have a poor income, then you go into a low bracket along with the high income earners who have certified they are poor.

The United States employs a progressive tax system, which means as your income grows, things get progressively more confusing. Above all, this is the land of opportunity, where everyone has chance to make a lot of money and get audited.

Guaranteed Guarantees

It has been said that death and taxes are the only guarantees in life. While remarkably creepy, this heavily repeated axiom is only partly correct. You see, with enough loopholes and creative accounting, a person can probably avoid paying most, if not all, of their taxes. But aside from that, it badly misses a third guarantee: aggravation.

The certainty of this assurance was experienced firsthand by one self-employed business owner who was asked to pay his taxes in quarterly installments.

"How do I know the correct amount in taxes I'm supposed to pay?" he wondered. "My income is sometimes up and sometimes down but never the same."

"You should pay your taxes based upon your estimated income," his accountant explained.

And so following his accountant's advice, that's what he did. He paid his taxes quarterly based upon his estimated income. Two years later he received a penalty notice from the IRS.

He was understandably angry, so, taking the matter into his own hands, he went directly to the IRS.

"Why am I being penalized for paying my income taxes?" he demanded to know.

Is getting flushed down the toilet
a taxable event?

It took a while, but, after passing through an extremely dangerous labyrinth known as an IRS call center, he finally got the answer.

"Penalties and interest are due, sir, because you estimated your taxes wrong," said the IRS.

Today this same gentlemen's income level still fluctuates all over the place, but his aggravation level remains quite steady.

Dependable Tax Deductions

One of the more confusing tax rules is the taxpayer exemption for dependents. This book will not take up the subject in great depth other than to say that household pets, no matter how cute, cannot be counted as dependents. Likewise, the IRS itself cannot be counted as a dependent on your tax return, although it is very much depending on you and a few hundred million other people for tax income.

Speaking of dependents, children generate large capital losses and are a wonderful tax deduction. Be fruitful and multiply! More times than not, the financial losses associated with raising children are so large that they will supersede the benefits of the tax write-off altogether.

Of course, even with the best tax deductions, many grey areas remain.

Take, for example, a $6,000 shower curtain. Is it a tax deductible expense, or not? I suppose if the shower curtain has a corporate logo affixed to it, there's an outside chance it's worthy of a deduction. On the other hand, if it's a see-through shower curtain, all bets are off.

Certain professionals on Wall Street have made a regular habit of having their clients bathe in the same tub as the $6,000 shower curtain. I don't know what tax auditors would say, but I think we can all agree that stinky clients are poor etiquette.

There are tons of other creative tax deductions that wonderfully skirt the rules. In the interest of good taste, I won't comment on the tax deductibility of ice sculptures that urinate vodka. Use your own sound judgment, even though I know you don't have any.

Tax Havens

Most of the notorious tax avoidance strategies have been thoroughly covered elsewhere; therefore, I want to share the lesser known techniques.

In recent years, renouncing a person's citizenship has become one method for minimizing taxes. This strategy is especially convenient for Big Shots who have mansions and villas scattered throughout the world. The differences between Europe's Mediterranean coast and Southern California's are minimal, with the exception of the double parked shopping carts at Venice Beach. Certain mavens have taken a few extra steps to assure themselves of a tax cut by completely renouncing their genetic link to humanity.

Vanishing into thin air is another tax skirting technique that is more complicated than it sounds. This method can involve various decoys— from faking your own death to taking up permanent residence in a vacant World War II bunker. I do not necessarily endorse the disappearing act as a tax avoidance strategy. Personally, I've never been attracted to the fugitive lifestyle, although I completely understand how it could appeal to an elite minority who prefer it over being cooped up in a glass office tower.

The $700 Million Man

Whatever tax losses a bear market is unable to create are effortlessly handled by the American public. This bumpy road was once traveled by a certain technology entrepreneur.

After selling his business to a corporate giant, the middle aged man netted an unbelievable amount and vowed never to work again. "If $700 million is not enough to take care of myself, along with my family and future generations, then I'm a stupid man," he reasoned. "How much money do you really need in life?"

Like many men of great wealth, his association with other wealthy individuals increased. He spent his money like them, and—even worse—he began to invest like them. His expansion into the thrilling arena of private equity, hedge funds, and venture capital, however, turned out to be not so thrilling. He burned through his first $100 million on personal expenses, leaving him with $600 million that was supposed to generate $60 million annually. To his chagrin, the $600 million turned into $300 million. What did he do to recoup his losses? He aggressively reinvested the $300 million, which quickly became $100 million. "If $100 million is not enough to make $300 million, then I'm a stupid man," he reasoned to himself. Without going into the gory details, his $100 million transformed itself into $7 million.

By that time, he was itching to get out of the office, so he went to his accountant's office to talk about it.

"Your tax losses can be carried forward to offset future capital gains," explained his cheerful accountant.

Staring at the wall, the $700 million man remained speechless. It had been a long time since he heard the phrase "capital gains," and while he didn't expect to have any, he most certainly liked the sound of it.

Other Tax Deductions

Is getting flushed down the toilet a taxable event? To find out, a vast multitude of people have put their money in ornate investment scams, and their market timing has been perfect. According to the IRS, very large tax deductions for losses from money put into Madoff schemes is now allowed.

These changes will be of particular interest for high net worth individuals desperately seeking reliable tax deductions. No longer will it be necessary to establish expensive and complicated tax shelters. Just jam your money into any suspicious investment con that regulators have yet to catch, and plunder away. Generous tax deductions await you.

Other categories of tax deductions include armored vehicles and corporate jets. Regarding armored vehicles, I believe they are a legitimate business expense, especially in the current economic environment, which has turned bloody. When the bull market returns, the armored vehicles can be exchanged for convertibles.

Dealing with Tax Audits

What should you do if you receive an IRS audit? Immediately stop everything you're doing. If you're in the hospital, get out. If you're working, quit. If you're on the verge of dying, postpone your death. If you're on vacation, come back. Drop everything. Likewise, moms and dads should give up parenthood until the audit is over.

How does a tax audit work? It begins with the IRS asking you to resubmit tax documentation they probably already have in their possession. The letter requesting your tax information will contain a submission deadline that has likely passed or is about to. The tax files you originally sent to the IRS are stored somewhere in the catacombs of their national or regional offices, but nobody wants to go down there to look. Usually, the requested tax documents are from several years ago, which means you probably don't have them anymore. And if you did keep them, then they most certainly can't be located. Save your paperwork.

By this time, the shock and outrage of being the focus of an IRS audit almost begins to set in. Next comes the back-and-forth interchange between you and them that goes nowhere fast. Each party sends the other party important correspondence that never gets received because the post office mishandles the mail. Save your paperwork.

Soon enough, the IRS' disorganization spreads and begins to infect you like a severe spatial disorder. You begin putting things where they don't belong. Your ex-spouse is renamed beneficiary on your life insurance. Your stocks and bonds are transferred into a college savings account for the benefit of your grandparents. Did I mention the importance of saving your paperwork?

Predictably,* the IRS' incompetence escalates like a hot IPO headed straight for the moon. Somebody owes somebody money; we just don't know who or how much. At this point, you'll most likely need professional help. I suggest enlisting the services of a properly qualified tax attorney or anyone else who fluently speaks the numeric-based language of form 1040. In the meantime, save your paperwork—all of it.

Becoming an IRS Auditor

Anybody looking for steady employment should consider becoming an IRS auditor. There are many benefits. Besides receiving a government paycheck, you have the authority to stalk people and to send them threatening letters. Under normal circumstances this type of behavior will almost immediately trigger a restraining order and cause you many legal anxieties—but not if you're an IRS auditor.

Not just anyone can become an IRS auditor. You will need to develop an incurable frown and not laugh at funny jokes. It also helps to be suspicious of all commercial activity, especially cash businesses and high income earners. You will begin your initial day of training by auditing your grandmother. If that sounds too harsh, you can start by interrogating her first and get to the audit later.

Finally, your official employee handbook will be *How to Lose Friends and Alienate People*, written by Irving D. Tressler. If you don't like to

---

*Did I just commit an unforgivable sin by using the word "predictable" in a financial book? Does the author have no shame?

read, you can order the audio book for $19.99. Don't be cheap. It's a tax deductible expense.

Relocating the Headquarters

Many businesses have been moved or established in offshore tax havens to minimize taxes. For instance, a number of reinsurance companies have migrated from the U.S. to Bermuda over the past several years. These headquarters are quite fitting, too, because the earnings and assets, like the vessels passing through the Bermuda Triangle, have disappeared.

No matter how unpatriotic it may seem to operate businesses a safe distance from U.S. shores, it's a misjudgment for the IRS or anyone else to assume that avoiding taxes is the only motivation for relocating. It is also done so that corporate executives can escape the hell of winter. You can't park a yacht on the Hudson River in the middle of January, can you?

Meeting the Tax Deadline: A Few Tips

As a convenience to the esteemed reader, I'd like to interrupt this chapter with a few important steps to help you pay your taxes in a timely fashion.

1) *Try using a calendar.* Individual income tax returns are due on April 15; however, when that date falls on Emancipation Day, another holiday, or the weekend, tax returns are due on the following business day.

2) *File your taxes electronically.* Thanks to the Internet, this particular method for tax payment has become very popular. The IRS notifies the taxpayer or tax preparer within 24 hours that it has received their e-filed return, and refunds can happen within a matter of weeks. Interestingly, this time frame is the same as an admission into a mental hospital from overexposure to online tax forms.

3) *File an extension.* This method for paying your taxes buys you more time to procrastinate. You'll also get to earn another few extra months of interest on the money you would've given to the IRS. Naturally, penalties and interest on any overdue taxes apply.

4) *Die on or before the tax deadline.* Another way to file your taxes on time, or better yet, not to deal with them at all, is to die on or before the tax deadline. Unfortunately, dying may still subject you to estate taxes and other miscellaneous expenses, so you may not necessarily be completely out of the woods. (Note: Death is the author's least favorite way of meeting the tax deadline.)

Finding a Good Beneficiary Part I

I sympathize with all moguls because nobody seems to understand that dismantling a vast empire can be a cumbersome chore. Where do you put it? To a certain degree, estate planning lawyers get it, but it's only because they're charging hourly rates. The relocation of an empire is an especially difficult task to undertake after years of persecuting everyone from business associates and competitors to neighbors and housekeepers. Even if someone could afford to buy it, who would want to?

For wealthy individuals with more enemies than friends who find themselves in this predicament, there's hope. I recently expanded my list of services. Along with donations, I'm now accepting inheritances. In addition, for a reasonable fee, I can also be your scapegoat or fall guy, just as long as no prison time is involved.

Unofficial Tax Reduction Strategies

Certain tax reduction strategies have no official name and can only be classified as "miscellaneous secrets." I came across this in my former capacity as a securities salesperson when I met a wealthy man whose net worth was so fantastic it caused his family a large tax liability. To address the problem, he hired an extensive team of tax experts, which excluded me.

They quickly designed an elaborate tax shelter that called for reporting zero income from over a thousand different places. But before they could initiate the plan, the tax laws were unexpectedly changed.

So the team of tax experts went back to the drawing board, this time re-crafting a formidable tax shelter by establishing multiple shell companies in order to generate substantial losses. But before they could implement the plan, the tax laws were unexpectedly changed again.

By this time, a year had passed, and the wealthy man's large tax liability had grown even larger. He called for a private meeting with his tax advisors, demanding to know what tax reduction strategies they had implemented. When he arrived for his appointment, he was greeted by an administrative assistant who handed him an envelope with a letter inside that read:

> *Dear Client,*
>
> *We're sorry to inform you that, due to tax law changes, we could not locate a suitable tax shelter for you. As a reimbursement for your losses, enclosed is our tax deductible invoice for $937,000.*
>
> *Yours truly,*
> *Flaygrant, Billings, Bait, Foil & Tackle, LLP*

Needless to say, the wealthy man wasn't happy with the letter, but he did receive a rather large tax deduction.

The ABCs of Estate Planning

Estate taxes are imposed upon the transfer of a deceased person's property to a designated beneficiary. This phenomenon takes place despite the fact that during the dead person's lifetime he probably paid many taxes to acquire those possessions. And, while estate taxes have been called a "death tax," I like to think of them as a going away gift to the government.

Although I'm not an estate planning specialist by trade, I do know a few burial strategies. For example, it's best to execute an estate plan when you are still alive. That's because being dead is a full-time job, which means you won't have any time to make decisions once it happens. Likewise, you will want to finish your estate plan *before* memory loss sets in and you forget who you are along with everybody else. At that point, it's probable you'll begin to confuse the federal government with family.

Ideally, a very large estate with no estate to speak of is the best estate planning strategy around. It's also fireproof because there's nothing left to burn, not to mention tax. Isn't this among the top reasons why Bill Gates and Warren Buffett decided to gift away their billions to charity? However, unlike them, most of us will never get the opportunity to bequeath our billions to charitable causes. That's because we've already discovered other ways to decimate our net worth to the point of where estate planning doesn't even matter. For a good portion of us, just having a funeral with flowers will be considered a victory.

Death vs. Taxes

There is one more tax law amendment you should be aware of. According to my sources, simplification of the tax code is scheduled to take effect next year on February 31st. Be sure to make a note.

In the end, it becomes all but obvious that death and taxes are among the most powerful forces in the natural world and—not far behind—is aggravation.

This taxing conclusion leaves us with just one final question: If death met taxes in a dark alley, who would win? Before answering, consider this: Death claims its victims only once. On the other hand, taxes will snag you every single year of your entire adult life.

Regardless of these disturbing facts, a gullible populace has been tricked into accepting the cozy idea of "good taxes." Warning: This is another one of those fake guarantees, along with harmless explosives, gourmet junk food, mild depression, and educated horse bets. The government is always on the prowl for new things to tax, and they usually get their way. Is a tax on breathing next?

Chapter 8
Cops and Robbers

"Too many of our stunt people are getting hurt!" complained one Hollywood executive. "If this keeps up, we won't have any healthy people left." So the desperate executive hired a risk consultant to advise his film company on what to do.

"How can we make diving head first out of a 40-story building safer?" asked the boss.

The consultant began to study the situation, and, after many months of careful analysis, an executable solution could not be identified. Before the contract was about to expire, the consultant approached the executive with a proposal to convert the filmmaker into a helmet company. The consultant's recommendation was greeted with great enthusiasm and everyone immediately felt safer.

Something similar happened on Wall Street.

Out of concern for the public's safety, it was determined that better securities rules and regulations were needed to prevent investors from becoming an endangered species. This lengthy process, decades in the making, eventually resulted in the formation of the Securities and Exchange Commission (SEC)—a Washington, D.C., based government agency responsible for policing Wall Street.

While it hasn't received much publicity, the SEC doesn't just function as Wall Street's sheriff; it also doubles as a famous playwright. The Act of 1933, the Act of 1934, and the Act of 1940 are among their most famous productions. Rumor has it they're hard at work on several unwanted sequels. It remains to be seen whether the new Acts will be categorized by legal critics as comedy, drama, or horror.

The General Idea

Maintaining orderly financial markets is among the SEC's top priorities. Although they were unable to effectively do this in 1973, 1987, 2008, or on May 6, 2010, the SEC is still trying. Merely stating that one is attempting to maintain orderliness serves other trivial purposes, namely to warn all disorderly market participants to stay far away. So if you're ever in the mood to crash someone's party, please make sure it's not the one located at 11 Wall Street or the one at 53rd and Broadway.

We cannot ignore the SEC's other goal: creating a fully-informed investing public.

Let's briefly consider what might occur if one incredible day the great masses arose from their slumbers to find themselves fully informed. Can you imagine what sort of chaos that would cause? Everyone, being fully informed, would know exactly whether to buy or sell, and, whichever it was, they would all try to do the same thing at the same time. Talk about mayhem! Who would execute the other side of the trade? That fateful day would most assuredly represent a death stroke to any conceptions of a "fair and orderly market." It's also a day whose contradictions regulatory idealists have yet to resolve.

Wanted Dead or Alive

In recent years, the SEC's pinnacle of regulatory success* is illustrated by its "big" catches.

Exhibit A: The crucifixion of Martha Stewart has the SEC's trademark stamped everywhere. She was convicted of lying to investigators about a stock sale that involved purposely avoiding $45,673 in market losses.

---

*Now that I have thoroughly blasphemed the word "success," what next?

Stewart served five months in prison, with limited access to flowers and baking pans. Because of her imprisonment, the SEC almost single-handedly starved our nation. How many cookie snacks were missed during Stewart's detention? I'm glad to report most Americans have gained back all the pounds they lost.

Exhibit B: Allen Stanford is another outstanding example of "big" catches. He was allowed to become a billionaire after many years of being secretly watched but never caught. All fingers point directly to the SEC's faulty license revocation policy. While the agency has revoked plenty of series 6s, 7s, and 24s, it has yet to revoke anybody's license to steal. To salute his financial acumen, Antigua and Barbuda knighted Stanford as an official "Sir." But in Texas, where he grew up, he's still known as "cattywompus."

Exhibit C: A final case study is none other than Bernard Madoff, whose multi-billion dollar investment scam to this day continues to awe crooks (and capitalists) throughout the world. According to some accounts, he became a millionaire by the age of 29 but only because he was a thief by the age of 16. The SEC, technically speaking, cannot count Madoff as a "big" catch, because they never caught him. He was ratted out by his sons. As a result, Madoff was found guilty and sentenced to 150 years behind bars, which is a pretty good deal. Did you know that in the Republic of Congo—for similar sins and offenses—they rope you to a tree and come back for you in three months? And if you're dead when they return, that means you escaped.

Stealing and Taking

As difficult as it may be for the general public to accept, outright fraud seldom appeals to the dishonest Wall Street mind. For one thing, fraud has no lengthy registration process, which gives the entire fraudulent act a strong odor of illegitimacy. More important, straightforward fraud is just too simple. There are countless other creative ways to steal money than to steal money.

Two examples that come to mind are: taking management fees of 1.5 percent from mutual fund shareholders for clumsy results, and taking a non-negotiable underwriting fee on a big IPO that never should been underwritten. Of course, these particular methods for taking what's not yours are just the tip of the iceberg. Happily, these daily occurrences go regularly unnoticed.

Inventing Rules – A Short Lesson

Pessimists say financial regulators have had so many big misses that they might as well not have existed. But this is a shortsighted view. It also fails to appreciate that creating a bureaucratic dynasty takes careful planning. Haven't regulators done a flawless job at creating a culture of crybabies and tattletales? To say they haven't done anything is not only unfair, but also untrue.

For whatever it's worth, here is the general order of all securities rulemaking: Previous rules are replaced with new rules, which eventually get replaced with the previous rules. Meanwhile, as a team of government lawyers continually adds to the cesspool of existing rules, an even larger team of lawyers working for Wall Street exploits the loopholes like a hot knife slicing through butter. And whatever loopholes *they* miss, lobbyists have already begun to tackle. Ultimately, innovative rules lead to innovative rule-skirting.

For the quantitative-oriented minds that still don't understand this concept, here's the equation:

Old Rules (x) + New Regulation (y) = More Rules^{10} (z)

More Rules^{10} (z) + Future Rules $(?)$ = More Rules and Laws^{100}

More Rules and Laws^{100} = More Loopholes ^{1000}

Mathematical equations aside, we are still left with two juicy questions: Is it against the law to break the rules when there are no rules? Do more rules create better regulation, or does more regulation create better rules?

Understanding the Mumbo Jumbo

A prospectus is the financial industry's version of chiaroscuro, where bold contrasts between light and dark are used to give the subject matter the perception of depth.

What is a prospectus? According to widely held views, it is a financial pamphlet that will make investors smarter, but I've never personally seen this great metamorphosis actually happen. Interestingly, the individuals making this argument also believe that reading a dictionary will induce a person to great wisdom.

What will you encounter inside a prospectus?

You will read about important matters like risk, fees, and that the fund company's P.O. Box address is located in Dubuque, IA, while its actual headquarters is over in Boston, MA. You will also read later paragraphs that disagree with former ones, and vice versa. But don't be alarmed; this confusing mess just means that securities lawyers are doing their jobs.

Several important enhancements to fund prospectuses have been made. The SEC now requires mutual fund companies to write the prospectus, along with risk factors, in plain English. Before this time, these sections were apparently only made available in Klingon and Pig Latin. In addition, I'm happy to report that the trial with shortened versions of the prospectus called "summary pages" has been a smashing success. Not a single complaint from the Professional Association of Speed Readers has yet been filed.

Here's another major change: Most fund prospectuses are now available as electronic documents instead of in printed form, meaning rainforests now have another ten good years before experiencing complete

This page intentionally left blank.

annihilation. It also means your computer's hard disk space is the only thing that gets wasted. If that's not progress, then what is?

Another area of the prospectus that needs discussion is the section that says "This page is intentionally left blank." This particular sentence speaks volumes and is not so much a disclosure as it is a tribute to minimal art.

The three most important words you'll come across in a prospectus are "May lose value." And as an addendum to these words, I think regulators should insert the following phrase, "Warning: This is not a toy."

As I discovered from my own experiences as a securities salesperson, a prospectus is more than just a thick volume enjoyed by *Beowulf* enthusiasts: It is a gigantic obstacle to getting new customers. I learned this lesson the hard way. After meeting with a prospect who wanted to buy a mutual fund, I could taste a sale coming. Then I made my closing pitch by telling him to read the prospectus. He responded by saying, "Let me get back to you in a week." That was the last time I ever heard from my prospect, and shortly thereafter, my love affair with the securities business abruptly ended.

Governing Thyself

The basic idea of "Self-Regulatory Organizations" (SROs) is that a government-designated group can self-govern the matters pertaining to its own business, which raises an important question: Who knows more about Wall Street's business? Is it the government, or Wall Street? I believe the correct answer is neither. In any case, I say it's best to err on the side of negligence. You see, Wall Street needs no meddling cops to help them mess up their businesses because they're quite capable of messing it up on their own. In that respect, the SRO experiment has been a wonderful model of success.

In 2007, the SEC approved a merger of the NYSE and the NASD. The combined entity gave birth to a new SRO called the "Financial Industry Regulatory Authority" or FINRA for short. Unbeknownst to its founding fathers, the creation of FINRA is a classic textbook example of just how far self-regulation has gone astray. Of what value is a pretty face without a pretty name?

Regarding FINRA's name, shouldn't the NASD have received more recognition? And what about the NYSE? And how could FINRA's organizers blatantly omit any references to the SEC? If this is self-regulation, then what is chaos? Errors of this nature at the self-regulatory level are a true travesty of justice and, if not, then they are an utter travesty in naming rights.

Crucial matters like the inspirational names behind cosmetic watch groups require better planning. As a matter of fairness, shouldn't everyone within the regulatory chain of command be recognized? Clearly, the FINRA name should have contained references to the NYSE, NASD, SRO, SEC, and, of course, the Police. I suggest something like NYSENASDSROSECPOLICE. If that's too long, then another authoritative-sounding acronym should immediately replace FINRA. What about NOPE?

History shows self-regulation is still very much a hit or miss exercise with many more misses than hits. Nevertheless, the SRO concept has proven to be quite successful* at helping other over-regulated businesses outside of the securities industry. The best example I can cite is the Italian mafia, who have been regulating themselves without police intervention for decades. I don't know how effective the mob's self-regulation has been, but so far nobody has complained.

---

*One more gross misusage of the word "successful" won't hurt anybody, will it?

*Does her bikini provide adequate disclosure or
does it require a statement of additional information?*

The Land of "No"

Nowhere within an investment firm is the word "no" heard more often per capita—besides the boardroom—than in the compliance department.

Compliance officers say "no" to the latest marketing campaign; they say "no" to disclosure verbiage; they say "no" to new product launches; and they say "no" to anyone who disagrees with "no." One of the few times they'll say "yes" is to compliance meetings.

For this reason, the compliance department is probably the most hated unit within any investment firm, aside from other divisions like legal, accounting, asset management, public relations, executive management, research, sales, and marketing. I know from my own personal experience that most compliance departments make it their duty to say "no" with such great frequency that the word "yes," when spoken, triggers company-wide shock.

Show and Tell

Large financial problems usually require a large response, but since a large response seldom happens, a small response usually has to suffice. In this particular regard, greater financial disclosure has become the SEC's favorite panacea to fixing whatever's broken on Wall Street. According to theory, whatever was going right went wrong because of inadequate disclosure.

There is much debate about what constitutes adequate disclosure. To resolve this matter, I suggest taking a field trip to your local beach. (A swimming pool of any kind with lots of people will suffice if there are no beaches where you live.) Now, without offending your fellow sunbathers, look around, and ask yourself: Does her bikini provide adequate disclosure, or does it require a statement of additional information? After completing this exercise, I think you'll agree that disclosure, like beauty, is in the eye of the beholder.

For this good reason and a thousand others, it is the author's view that more disclosure does very little to prevent crime. Don't the best thieves fully disclose their robberies right before taking off with the stolen loot? As a matter of fact, this happened in 1911, just as the Mona Lisa was being stolen from the Louvre. The thief quietly muttered, "Give me the painting and nobody gets hurt." As it turns out, no one realized the masterpiece was missing until the following day. Even though a full disclosure preceded the crime, the criminal act invalidated the kindness of the legal notice.

In the end, disclosure is equivalent to some show and some tell, but much more show than tell.

Timing the Market

The SEC's close association with Wall Street has rubbed off in a least one more verifiable manner: the SEC's market timing is awful. For regulators, inventing rules for problems that no longer exist not only comes as second nature, but invention has become a mainstay.

This point is best illustrated by the SEC's rule to ban naked short selling. As we've been told, this particular trade is so evil that it is on par with the rape of Lucretia. But just as this particular rule went into effect, day trading went back to being a hobby. By the time the rule was made law, anyone it would have applied to who had a significant chunk to gamble had all but disappeared.

Short-sellers who are betting a stock is going to fall will borrow a company's shares, sell them and buy them back at lower prices when the stock falls. They profit by sticking the lower priced shares back to the lender. Champagne, anyone? As good as that sounds, a more frequent occurrence is that short-sellers get stuck with losses—lots of them. But no one sees this happening because only the short-sellers and the IRS are keeping track.

In the case of naked short-selling, traders were once able to sell shares they neither owned nor borrowed. Before you yell, "Sign me up," we can't, because applications to Club Naked have been outlawed.

As a result, the obituary for naked short-selling reads like this:

> *All public nudity in the capital markets shall never again be tolerated, unless by private exception you happen to be super big, super hot, or both.**

Why this prohibition was not already in place is still not known, but the matter is being carefully studied by legal students who will eventually go into family law.

Catching the Crooks

Many of us are rightly suspicious of the entire regulatory system that was purportedly established for our protection. And the worker exchange program between Wall Street and the SEC has done little to quell these suspicions.

Worse yet, it has been suggested** that the SEC is secretly acting in collusion with Wall Street. Given how certain things have strangely disappeared while other things have never appeared, it's hard to disagree. What if the bad guys have already infiltrated the police force? Is it a remote possibility? How can you catch the crooks when you *are* the crooks? These are all perfectly legitimate questions that I refuse to answer mainly out of concern for my personal safety.

Although this section started out with the sub-heading "Catching the Crooks," I never indicated that the crooks would actually be caught or convicted or actually serve time or pay a meaningful penalty; it was only

---

*See Treasury STRIPS.
**Not by me.

*...and deliver us please from the oppressive scarecrows
that try to regulate us.*

suggested as a possible outcome. I apologize if you're not happy with that cop-out.

Manipulating the Market

Manipulation refers to the dishonest activity by individuals or institutions who try to game the price of a stock or a certain market for their own financial gain. Wall Street, in its constant pledge to innovate, has introduced various versions of manipulation, like pumping and dumping, bear raiding, and painting the tape. There's no sense in naming specific manipulators or their ghastly deeds, because tomorrow's generation of gypsters will no doubt surpass them.

The Securities Exchange Act of 1934 Section 9 strictly prohibits *all* securities manipulation. There are no ifs, ands, or buts about the application of this rule, and even the least seasoned Wall Streeter knows it. Nobody is above the law, allegedly. Yet it has come to the author's belated attention that the very police force that invented this rule is in violation.

Are not regulators who ban legitimate short selling, for whatever reasons, breaking their own rules by creating a rigged one-way market with artificially inflated prices? If that's not the definition of market manipulation, what is? And what can be said about similar efforts like Operation Twist or the mysterious existence of the Plunge Protection Team?

As you can see, our innocent foray into securities law has gone from a simple inquiry into a complicated web of moral issues. Why do securities rules apply to everyone but the police? How can a "free market" without underhanded interference really be free, if it isn't free? Are the police really police? Who's policing the police?

Becoming the Ringleader

There are many people who believe they can do a better job of supervising Wall Street than the SEC, just as there are many people who believe they make a better quarterback for the Cleveland Browns than the current man. Are you one of them? Do you think you have what it takes to become an SEC Commissioner?

Before your suitability for the job can be determined, you will need to be properly screened.

First, you should understand there are actually *five* Commissioners. Which one would you like to be? If you answered, "Chairman," you're already well ahead of the other job candidates. If you were slow to answer the question, or didn't answer at all, how can you become the boss if you don't know who the boss is?

Next, you'll need to understand the level of office we're talking about. Each Commissioner is a Presidential appointee. That means if you want to become the next acting Commissioner, you need to have a job interview with the President of the United States!

If you're still undeterred, your boot camp training has already started. Please send your resume directly to the White House and be sure to indicate how many big-time crooks you've apprehended over the past six months. If you haven't caught more than two, you can still apply for the position, but frisking suspects doesn't count.

While you wait for your rejection letter to arrive, here's your next assignment: Enter any Federal building and you must pass through the security checkpoint's metal detectors with keys in your pocket. (No plastic keys are allowed.)

Should you succeed, a bright future in securities law enforcement awaits you. Remember: To enforce the law, you must first be able to successfully break it without being detected. Nowhere does this ring truer than on Wall Street, where undetected activity is not just the hallmark of all great criminals but also of great policemen.

On a Positive Note...

To a greater extent, I think today's police work has become a modern day replica of the Spanish Inquisition. In some cases it appears the SEC has completely shifted its attention away from regulating to revenge. Someday all of this may eventually lead to one worldwide regulator that combines Interpol, the CIA, FINRA, SEC, and SWAT under one united offense against anyone wearing a Brooks Brothers suit.

On the other hand, there's a very strong case to be made that Wall Street's financial regulators aren't even police but are mere babysitters, and not very good ones. For sure, the SEC has contributed to a sharp increase in paranoia from within Wall Street's ranks, but here too is a silver lining: It has provided psychiatrists with a steady flow of new patients, which has boosted national GDP by 0.00012 percent.

There will always be a hopeless constituency that believes the SEC is at fault for all of the times they've been robbed or lost money. It never occurs to them that disorderly-placed investments or putting money with financial perverts leads to perverted results.

From what I gather, most of Wall Street's criminals have already been barred from the securities business, or they've graduated to bigger things, like how to run the world. The rest of their time is spent sheltering their billions in private offshore charities. Thankfully they are no longer the SEC's concern because they now fall under the dual jurisdiction of the IRS and Coast Guard.

Admonition and a Word of Thanks

For the public good, I would like to see the SEC simplify its charter and aim for more achievable milestones. How about this one: "We won't make things worse." Now there's a bona fide mission statement, and it even has a nice ring to it.

In the meantime, I offer my deepest sympathies to all the investment businesses that have thrived during an era of limited government intervention but now face greater scrutiny. Like Rip Van Winkle, you've awakened to an unfamiliar place with unfamiliar rules, and the age of anything goes is over. To all the capitalist hippies in this predicament, I offer this admonition: Don't be a prude, dude. Give regulation a chance.

I know there's a growing populace who would like to abolish the SEC, and they have a point. No existence is better than an ineffective existence—isn't it? I liken the SEC's existence to the feathers on an ostrich. Do an ostrich's feathers help it to fly better? Not really, but like the SEC, the feathers are there for decorative purposes. Can you imagine what an already ugly beast would look like without feathers?

If you're currently registered with the SEC or anybody like it, I would like to thank you for your token gesture of cooperation. Your membership fees will go a long way to helping the agency stay afloat for at least another six months.

In summary, financial regulators need no further advice on how to administer their affairs, because their body of work speaks for itself. The sad reality is that stupidity cannot be regulated, and all practical efforts to govern Wall Street have had about the same level of success* as subduing Mount Vesuvius.

Out of self-defense, I neither admit nor deny that I had anything to do with this chapter.

---

*This time I really mean it. Cross my heart.

Chapter 9
Somewhere Over
the Rainbow

My fellow citizens, please accept my apologies for the previous eight chapters. I got carried away. Some of you will be delighted to know that this particular chapter has been reduced in order to eliminate overhead. Due to this unexpected event (no doubt, a swarm of Black Pianos from the sky), I will try to compensate the reader with more financial information, but in fewer words. As they say in baseball, "I'll be swinging for the fences!"

In Chapter One, I promised to provide you with a market update on the $35,000 toilet and the $6,000 shower curtain. Regrettably, I'm unable to do that because this book is a bear market edition, and those items were acquired during a bull market. Additionally, the individuals who did the acquiring flunked Benjamin Graham's school of value investing. Nonetheless, if market conditions change, we can probably reopen the matter, but don't count on it.

...Second Thoughts

I'd like to refute a statement I made earlier. I suggested that dart-throwing monkeys could effortlessly outperform a portfolio of securities managed by professionals. That assertion has only been true 98.8 percent of the time

During the boom years, certain investment managers used leverage to amplify their gains, giving onlookers the deceptive appearance that they were "managing risk." The only reason these managers looked better than the rest of the market was because they were taking on more risk. But when the stock market crashed, they did too. To this day, some of them remain in business, selling themselves as experts in "risk reduction." All along, the only financial risk they've been reducing is their own— away from poverty. Meanwhile, client fees continue paying for the entire experiment.

At the opposite extreme of these financial acrobats are the Hyper-conservative Chickens. This latter group puts their clients' money in a safe place with a low return. This type of investment manager gives himself a back-pat for earning the clients an honest half percent and not stealing from them. He claims that stocks are too dangerous to touch right now. He keeps the portfolio in cash equivalents to reduce market volatility. He says he must act with prudence, because, if he doesn't, the family's army of lawyers will burn him at the stake. He overstates his case, with the exception of the part about being burnt at the stake by lawyers.

In addition to the Hyper-conservative Chicken there is another fascinating creature called the Financial Chameleon. This particular mammal can instantly change its color depending on the sunlight's direction. It is hard to pin down a Chameleon and even harder to catch. Can you guess which of these conditions the author suffers from?

A Little Pep Talk

I'd like to share with you an investment plan that withstands the test of time by not only preserving your net worth but also substantially growing it. Here it is:

During a bull market, when everyone is chasing stocks, gather up all your stocks and sell them. Then, redeploy the money into low risk bonds. What if the stocks you just sold skyrocket? This too shall pass;

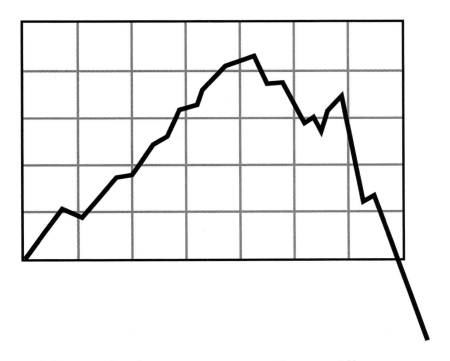

This may be the most important chart you'll ever see.
Please memorize it.

so ignore it and go about your business. Sooner or later a depression will come, and, when it does, you'll be ready. After the depression turns into a full-fledged global crisis, sell your bonds and repurchase stocks. What if the stocks you just re-bought sink like quicksand? This too shall pass; so ignore it and go about your business. Patiently wait for the next bull market to arrive, and, when it does, you'll be ready. By repeating this process throughout your lifetime, you'll end up with more money than you'll ever need.

A closer look at financial history shows this advice worked remarkably well for anyone with enough moxie to have followed it. The main problem, however, is mental. Our natural propensity is to follow the crowd's behavior. Nobody wants to sell stocks that are universally loved in order to buy bonds that everyone hates. As odd as it may seem, there's an elite constituency who actually invests in this most unusual way. Although I've never personally met them, I've been told their personal wealth rivals Bolivia's GDP.

I completely understand that it is difficult to accept the possibility of anyone buying unpopular investments consistently, let alone one time. With the media's help, the public is given the false idea that on a day of spectacular selling, there were no buyers. This, of course, is completely untrue. If the selling volume on that horrendous day consisted of five billion, three hundred and fifty-four million, seven hundred thousand shares, the buying volume can easily be computed. In this particular case it was 5,354,700,000.

When Were the "Good Old Days?"

In an effort to find out what was good during the good old days, we must first determine when specifically the good old days were. In some Wall Street minds, the good old days were any days before the Sarbanes-Oxley Act, or other equally unpleasant legislation. There's a profound yearning for the nostalgic years when the most vital securities rules were: "Don't take continuing education courses for other people," "Pay your annual registration fees on or before the due date," and "Always deliver a prospectus containing information about the same securities you discussed with the client."

For the rest of us, especially anybody who says "I miss the good old days," I have a question for you: Which good old days are you referring to?

Are you thinking about the good old days of fuel shortages in the 1970s? Or maybe you mean the good old days of 20 percent interest rates in the early 1980s, when it was cheaper to borrow money from the Mafia than your local bank. Is that it? Or, perhaps, you covet the good old days of hot IPOs during the 1990s that made everyone rich but you. Or, maybe you miss that tumultuous period from 2000-09 when U.S. stocks gave you a big fat goose egg. Is that what you're longing for? Or, do you miss the multi-billion-dollar Wall Street bailouts, while you lost your job and house? Do you miss the good old days of 2010-11 when your cash investments were yielding close to zero percent? Which of these "good old days" do you crave?

In other minds, the "good old days" were when atomic bombs were built by mad scientists instead of mad 27-year-old MBAs with algorithms. Personally, I long for the days when private equity wasn't a public nuisance. Ah, those were the days! But I still don't know if they were any good.

Some Audience Participation

There's not a practicing economist, blogger, financial advisor, or inquisitive human from here to Waterloo who doesn't have an opinion on how to fix things. And, at the opposite spectrum is another very large audience, roughly about the same size, that thinks no fixing of anything is required. Long live the status quo!

Without belaboring the topic of fiscal shenanigans and general incompetence any more than I already have, I think it's only fair to allow the reader to chime in and offer some constructive criticism—and at the very least—some cheap shots.

To that end, the blank space below can be used to write whatever you please. You can be in favor of, or against everything, or both. If you need more space, I suggest you find a clean alley wall, or, worse yet, write a book.

_____

_____

_____

_____

_____

Causes and Effects

Let's revisit a dramatic point in stock market trading: May 6, 2010—a historical moment that probably never should have happened. Toward the market close on that fateful day, many dreadful things took place, the sorts of supernatural occurrences that, because of watchful regulation, aren't supposed to occur.

At 2:42 p.m., the Dow Jones Industrial Average was down a glum 300 points but within a matter of minutes managed to sink a frightful 998 points. A 600 point plunge within such a short span, while very bad, only scratches the surface. Among the magnificent transactions that took place were trades of just a few cents in stocks like Accenture and Procter & Gamble, while shares in other companies like Apple and Sotheby's shot past $100,000. Legitimate orders that never should been canceled got canceled, and illegitimate orders that never should have been filled were filled. Need we say more?

We already know about the harmful effects of wild days like these on us—permanent hair loss, premature wrinkles, heart conditions, nervous breakdowns, and so forth. But what about the precise causes of these troubling events? A 104-page essay by regulators attempted to answer this question, but, like Major League Baseball's Steroid Report, it struck out. No doubt a sequel report by them or any other brave takers is in the works.

A few vexing questions are raised:

1) Jeepers—these sorts of things still happen?

2) Why did regulators blame a single $4 billion order submitted on another securities exchange for the temporary disappearance of $1 trillion in market value? There's no denying $4 billion is a lot of bananas, but is that all it takes to play magic tricks with a trillion dollars? If so, who can we coax into lending us $4 billion?

3) Won't some compassionate stock market specialists please give us another chance at buying Procter & Gamble, or something similar, for pennies on the dollar? Pretty please?

4) The next time something of this magnitude happens, can we get the Chinese gongs, circuit breakers, ambulance sirens, fire alarms, time-out buzzers, text alerts, whistle blowers, and wedding bells to simultaneously broadcast a notice? Is that asking too much?

5) What do we do with the invoice from our failed EKG report? I recommend sending it directly to:
   SEC Headquarters / Attn: Chairman
   100 F Street, NE
   Washington, DC 20549

Our Special Report: Risk and Reward

As we've seen, managing and controlling financial risk is not Wall Street's forte. Most of the time, everything is perfectly normal until the unforeseen day when it's suddenly not. According to my estimates, computerized risk models are half the problem while the psychopaths programming them are the other 90 percent. Whatever billions these mighty algorithms effortlessly create, they also swiftly destroy. Who can blame the market for throwing an occasional temper tantrum? Wouldn't you do the same thing if people kept insisting they know what your very next move is going to be?

For readers who have not yet found within these pages a suitable investment program, I've located another plan that may interest you. Whatever it lacks in substance is fully reimbursed in creativity. The plan was explained to me by a successful* hedge fund manager. We had been discussing Modern Portfolio Theory—a boring subject. For 25 years he traded other people's money. His own money was mindfully buried in an offshore trust.

I finally told him, "Enough with your philosophical nonsense! If you were down to your last million, what would you do with it?"

"You put 98 percent of your investments in ultra-safe U.S. government bonds, while the remaining portion is carefully allocated in highly speculative bets," he answered. "Each of these bets is diversified across different areas, so all you need is for one small gamble to have a huge payout, and you're home free. The winning trade will more than make up for all the failed ones because, even if all the speculative trades blow up, you'd still have 98 percent of your money earning a modest income in low-risk government bonds. What's wrong with that?"

---

*I guarantee this will definitely be the final time I use this devilishly fun word in the book.

Financial games, continued:
Find the Jackpot.

Although I honestly believe this fund manager's hypothesis was well-intentioned, it's still a gross misapplication of everything he probably learned in Portfolio School. I think he was mixed up about which of his bets were speculative and which were not, but his strategy worked like a charm until the day that U.S. government bonds...

Forward-Looking Statements

Thus far I've avoided making any bold predictions, but the urge has overtaken me. Besides, I strongly object to playing second fiddle to the Bright Minds behind forecasts of Dow minus 4,000. So, from this point forward, I'm going for the gusto!

To regain my first mover advantage, here is my exact market forecast for the next 15 years:

Soaring interest rates
Plunging interest rates
Several market crashes
Several market recoveries
People will panic
People will celebrate
Real estate booms
Real estate busts
Oil shortages
Oil oversupply
Budget deficits
Budget surpluses
Many new companies
Many bankrupt companies
Many corrupt companies
Many corrupt politicians
Periods of inflation

Periods of deflation

Greedy bankers and other corporate types

Democratic controlled governments

Republican controlled governments

Military controlled governments

Madoff schemes

Many wars

Tax hikes

Wealth creation

Wealth destruction

Protesting in the streets

Please note the above mentioned events aren't necessarily listed in chronological order, unless they happen to occur in that manner. My risk model also assumes long periods of uncertainty.

As for the exact timing of these specific events, I have a penetrating hunch they will occur on Monday, Tuesday, Wednesday, Thursday, or Friday. If they don't, then it will definitely be on a Saturday or Sunday.

Finding a Beneficiary, Part II

In Chapter Seven, I floated the generous idea of me being the voluntary beneficiary for any wealthy individuals with a large estate. Not only am I the antithesis of your bratty, unappreciative heirs, but I know how to carefully spend a fortune. To those who reject this humanitarian offer, I will share with you another novel idea, because my loss is your gain.

Prior to her demise, a real estate tycoon bequeathed $12 million to a cute little doggie.* Her family wasn't happy with the decision, but that's just the tip of the iceberg. To the shocking dissatisfaction of canines everywhere, the bank refused to honor the inheritance check because

---

*This was done to keep up with the rising cost of dog mansions, doggie divorce court, and vegan ALPO.

it was endorsed with a paw print. Although banking regulations do allow for signature endorsements by sharks, wolves and snakes, there are no such provisions for toy poodles. The shortcomings of our banking system, which were supposedly contained, have now invaded the animal kingdom. Years ago Edward Abbey observed this trend: "When a man's best friend is his dog, that dog has a problem."

Guaranteed Investment Results

This book has not succeeded unless it has unmistakably communicated that the best way to avoid market losses is to not incur them. This pesky little reminder should never leave a person's cerebrum, regardless of how dazzling ticker symbol "SCKR" looks. Whatever you do, don't buy it! I understand that, for some of us, this simple-minded explanation of how to avoid losses is wholly unsatisfactory. So, I'll use another far-fetched, but precise, analogy: Contraceptives, also known as "birth control."

According to fertility experts, no two forms of birth control will ever work the same. Some methods are just as ineffective as the next, which is well illustrated by the densely populated crosswalks near Wall Street and its global suburbs, including China's Beijing Financial Street, England's Canary Wharf, India's Dalal Street, France's La Défense, Brazil's Avenida Paulista, and Japan's Kabutocho. In this regard, the only sure fire way to prevent gains (in your family's population) is coincidently the identical method to prevent losses (in your investment portfolio): Abstinence!

Closing Arguments

The conventional conclusion for most business and financial literature is to suggest solutions to all the problems that ail us. Toward the end of the book is a list of enlightening recommendations labeled something like "Wealth Secrets," "Financial Security," and "Necessary Steps toward Achieving Endless Prosperity." Somewhere in the mix there might even be a pushy invitation to attend the author's next workshop. (The lesser ambitious books will serve up a few outdated model investment portfolios.) It is wrongly presumed that the people who can articulate all the problems have all the answers.

Although the author of this book has never professed to have all the answers, or even some of them, he'd like to nonetheless take a swing at a few brainteasers, like:

1) Is capitalism doomed?

2) What do the charts say?

3) How can our financial problems be solved?

4) What stocks, ETFs, or other hot investments can be churned for a quick profit to pay for mama's dentures and papa's diapers?

In response to the first problem, the people who know everything there is to know about capitalism argue that the movement should return to its roots. And then there's the other group that knows nothing about capitalism, like Vladimir Lenin. He reportedly told his comrades, "The last capitalist will be hung with the rope he sells."

As sinister as that statement seems, it is immensely incomplete. Shouldn't Vlady have said something about what happens to all of the other capitalists before the last capitalist is hung? For example, do they get sued and go bankrupt shortly before their deaths? Do their assets get frozen and seized by authorities before they expire? Maybe the Chinese-made rope never makes it to dry land, allowing the capitalist who profited from its sale to narrowly escape. Another possibility is that the rope Vlady refers to is not really a rope, but a necktie. I suppose Lenin was too busy dodging his assassins to tell us.

A few alternatives to capitalism include feudalism or anarchy, which, no doubt, a number of individuals would like to give another try. Usually, these are the same people who feel cheated by any earthly possessions you've cobbled together through work, ingenuity and sweat.

Divine arrangements aside, we are backed into a corner for finding a better imperfect method for raising capital. Thus far, the only plausible system for extracting billions from the public and transferring it to corporations, for whatever purposes, is something similar to Wall Street's nefarious jalopy. (At times throughout history, money has been gathered from citizens by shooting tear gas into a public crowd, but the results have always been less than favorable.)

As to the question of what the charts are saying at this precise moment, we didn't care about that before, so why should we start caring now? And besides, the charts have always had a mind of their own. Forget about their lengthy interpretations and pay special attention to the sharply descending line that skips off the grid. Please memorize it.

Regarding problem three, some have taken the viewpoint that if whatever financial problems exist are broken, don't fix them. I once had an investment client who agreed with this view, and, although I don't think it was the right philosophy, I deeply admired her resilience to financial pain. I repeat: these kinds of people don't need a better investment plan; they need a straitjacket and a prescription for Prozac.

The solution to problem number four is an easy fix. Simply give us your credit card number, and, within 24 hours or less, a list of super hot picks will be sent to your email inbox. If you send money right away, a bonus list of investments to avoid will be included.

In summary, let me remind you that I'm still connected from an unsafe distance to Wall Street, but you have my full guarantee that I and my organization are nothing like the people or the places you just read about within these pages. Unlike them, we are principals with principles.

Whether you believe me or not, I know you're still searching for a comprehensive investment plan that offers both rapid growth and safety of capital. Boy, have I got the plan just for you! It should serve you well during bull markets and especially bear markets. It also provides smooth sailing through long periods of inflation, deflation, and any other berserk scenarios you can imagine. Whenever you're available, we can discuss the plan over lunch at the Four Seasons—you're buying.

In the meantime, all other inquiries are being handled by my legal counsel at Fish, Weasel & Skunk. If no one answers, just leave a message.